Index to
CHILDREN'S PLAYS
IN COLLECTIONS
1975-1984

by

Beverly Robin Trefny

and

Eileen C. Palmer

The Scarecrow Press, Inc.
Metuchen, N.J., and London
1986

Library of Congress Cataloging-in-Publication Data

Trefny, Beverly Robin, 1945–
  Index to children's plays in collections.

  Bibliography: p.
  Rev. ed. of: Index to children's plays in collections /
by Barbara A. Kreider. 2nd ed. 1977.
  1. Children's plays—Indexes. I. Palmer, Eileen C.
II. Kreider, Barbara A. Index to children's plays
in collections. III. Title.
PN1627.T73 1986   016.80882   86-6418
ISBN 0-8108-1893-0

ACKNOWLEDGMENTS

The editors are grateful that they still have family and friends after completing this book.

CONTENTS

INTRODUCTION / GUIDE TO USE

This third volume of the Index to Children's Plays in Collections expands upon the two previous ones with a wide diversity of dramatic literature for children including skits, monologs, one act plays, pantomimes, puppetry, and variety programs when in play form. This volume is comprised of 540 plays from 48 collections. When combined with the two previous volumes by Barbara Kreider (1972, 1977), this brings the total number of plays contained in Index to Children's Plays in Collections to 1990.

The following bibliographies were utilized by the editors in locating play collections published between 1975-84: Books in Print (R.R. Bowker Co., 1976-85 volumes), and the Elementary School Library Collection (Bro-Dart Foundation, 14th edition, 1984). All available play collections with copyright dates between 1975-84 are indexed. The emphasis is on inclusivity without regard to merit. The authors, titles, and subjects of all plays are included in one alphabet.

Sample author entry:

> Bradley, Virginia. If You Recognize Me, Don't Admit It. In Bradley, V. Is There an Actor in the House?
> 20+ char

This entry indicates that Virginia Bradley wrote the play entitled "If You Recognize Me, Don't Admit It"; that this play appears in the collection Is There an Actor in the House?, written by Virginia Bradley, and that the play has 20 characters and extras. "Extras" include nonspeaking characters, characters listed in groups, and both singing and speaking choruses.

Sample title entry:

Moonlife 2069. Henderson, N.

This entry indicates that the play entitled "Moonlife 2069" was written by N. Henderson.

Sample subject entry:

SANTA CLAUS
    Miller, P. Christmas at the O.K. Corral

This entry indicates that the subject "SANTA CLAUS" is treated in P. Miller's play, "Christmas at the O.K. Corral."

The user should note that the "subjects" chosen under which to arrange the various plays in the Index proper are not limited strictly to subjects but also include the following: themes, e.g., BROTHERHOOD; type of play, e.g., MELO-DRAMA or MYSTERY; occasion for which play was written, e.g., APRIL FOOL'S DAY or THANKSGIVING; period in which play was set, e.g., REVOLUTIONARY WAR (AMERICAN); set-ting (geographical) of a play, e.g., FRANCE; historical or legendary person involved, e.g., KING, MARTIN LUTHER; special cast, e.g., GIRL SCOUTS; and genre, e.g., PANTO-MIME.

For the benefit of those users who wish to browse for an idea, a summary listing of subject headings is provided beginning on page xi. Subjects for plays which have been given differing interpretations by various adaptors list the adaptor as author. Cross referencing is used in the subject index when appropriate.

Following the Index proper is the Cast Analysis section, in which the plays are arranged by the numbers of characters involved. This section is divided into four types of cast: all-female, all-male, mixed casts, and puppet plays. Under each of these four types the arrangement is from few to many characters by specific number. Further, entries under a sub-arrangement such as 3 characters are immediately followed by entries under the sub-arrangement 3 characters and extras. Adaptations are listed under the adaptor rather than the ori-ginal author in the cast analysis. When it is optional as to whether the cast consists of a single sex or mixed cast, entries are given for both.

The concluding portions of the <u>Index</u> are devoted to a Directory of Publishers which gives complete names and addresses for publishers whose collections are analyzed, and a Bibliography which contains full publication data plus grade-level indicators for all collections indexed.

SUMMARY OF SUBJECT HEADINGS

Actors and actresses
Adams, John
Adventure
Africa
Airports
Alphabet
American Indian Week
Animals
Apples
Appleseed, Johnny
April Fool's Day
Arabia
Arabian Nights
Archery
Arizona
Art
Artists
Asia
Astrology
Astronauts
Austria
Automobiles
Autumn

Babies
Babysitters
Baghdad
Baseball
Basketball
Beauty
Betting
Bible
Birds
Birthdays
Black Americans
Black History Week
Blackwell, Elizabeth
Blindness
Boasting

Book Week
Books
Bookworms
Boston Tea Party
Boy Scouts
Bravery
Brotherhood
Buddha
Buildings
Bunker Hill
Burma
Butterflies

Caesar, Julius
Calamity Jane
Careers
Castles
Cats
Chanukah
Children
China
Chinese New Year
Choral Plays
Christmas
Christmas Carols
Christmas Customs
Christmas in Other Countries
Christmas Trees
Circus
Civil Rights
Civil War
Cleverness
Clowns
Clubs (Associations)
Codes
Coins
Columbus, Christopher
Columbus Day
Comedy

THE INDEX

_____. _____. In Kamerman, S. A Treasury of Christmas
    Plays. 9 char
_____. A Merry Christmas. In Kamerman, S., On Stage for
    Christmas. 9 char
Alexander, Sue. The Case of the Kidnapped Nephew. In Alexand-
    er, S. Whatever Happened to Uncle Albert? 9 char
_____. Come Quick! In Alexander, S. Small Plays for Special
    Days. 2 char
_____. The Ghost of Plymouth Castle. In Alexander, S. What-
    ever Happened to Uncle Albert? 7 char
_____. Good Day, Giant! In Alexander, S. Small Plays for
    Special Days. 2 char
_____. Meow! and Arf! In Alexander, S. Small Plays for Spe-
    cial Days. 2 char
_____. Mystery of the Stone Statues. In Alexander, S. What-
    ever Happened to Uncle Albert? 5 char
_____. One, Two, Three! In Alexander, S. Small Plays for
    Special Days. 2 char
_____. Roar! Said the Lion. In Alexander, S. Small Plays for
    Special Days. 2 char
_____. Something Scary. In Alexander, S. Small Plays for Spe-
    cial Days. 2 char
_____. Tricky Gifts. In Alexander, S. Small Plays for Special
    Days. 2 char
_____. Whatever Happened to Uncle Albert? In Alexander, S.
    Whatever Happened to Uncle Albert? 5 char
Ali Baba and the 40 Thieves. Mahlmann, L.
All Because of a Scullery Maid. Phillips, M.
ALPHABET
    Bauman, A. Santa's Alphabet
Amateur Night at Cucumber Center. Bradley, V.
AMERICAN INDIAN WEEK
    Henderson, N. Little Turtle
Amos, Man from Takoah. Rembrandt, E.
Ananse's Trick Does Double Work. Korty, C.
Anansi and the Box of Stories. Mahlmann, L.
Anansi, the African Spider. Winther, B.
And Brings Us to This Season. Rembrandt, E.
And Christmas Is Its Name. Nolan, P.
Andersen, Hans C. The Emperor's New Clothes. In Lynch-Watson,
    J. The Shadow Puppet Book. 9+ char
_____. The Emperor's Nightingale. In Mahlmann, L. and D.
    Jones. Puppet Plays from Favorite Stories. 8 char
Anderson, Robert A. Panic in Space. In Kamerman, S. Space and
    Science Fiction Plays for Young People. 8 char
Androcles and the Lion. Harris, A.
ANIMALS
    Alexander, S. Come Quick!
    Carlson, B. Crowded?
    _____. The Law of the Jungle
    _____. Lion, Sick and Dying

_____. The Tiger, the Brahman, and the Jackal
_____. The Whole Truth
Cavannah, F. Mr. Bunny's Prize
Farrar, J. The Garden at the Zoo
Korty, C. Ananse's Trick Does Double Work
_____. The Man Who Loved to Laugh
_____. Mr. Hare Takes Mr. Leopard for a Ride
Lynch-Watson, J. The Little Red Hen
Mahlmann, L. Aesop's Fables
_____. The Elephant's Child
_____. The Gingerbread Boy
_____. King of the Golden River
_____. The Little Indian Brave
_____. The Rabbit Who Wanted Red Wings
_____. Tale of Peter Rabbit
Nolan, P. Stanislaw and the Wolf
Sergel, K. Winnie-the-Pooh
Winther, B. African Trio
_____. Anansi, the African Spider
_____. Ijapa, the Tortoise
_____. Little Mouse-Deer
_____. The Monkey Without a Tail
_____. Pacca, the Little Bowman
Anyone Could, but--. Carlson, B.
APPLES
    Bradley, V. Apples for Sale
    Nolan, P. Johnny Appleseed
Apples for Sale. Bradley, V.
APPLESEED, JOHNNY
    Bradley, V. If the Rabbit Pickets, You're Doing Something
        Wrong
    Harris, A. Yankee Doodle Dandies
APRIL FOOL'S DAY
    Alexander, S. Come quick!
    Bradley, V. Off Guard
    _____. Surprise
ARABIA
    Mahlmann, L. Aladdin, or The Wonderful Lamp
    _____. Ali Baba and the Forty Thieves
ARABIAN NIGHTS
    Winther, B. The Flying Horse Machine
ARCHERY
    Mason, T. Robin Hood: A Story of the Forest
    Nolan, P. Robin Hood and the Match at Nottingham
    _____. The Son of William Tell
ARIZONA
    Bradley, V. Arizona Pilgrims
Arizona Pilgrims. Bradley, V.
The Arrival of Paddington. Bradley, A.
ART
    Murray, J. For Art's Sake

_____. An International Affair
ARTISTS
        Miller, H. Season's Greetings
ASIA
        Winther, B. Prince Rama
Ask Mr. Jefferson. Fisher, A.
ASTROLOGY
        Murray, J. Flight International
ASTRONAUTS
        Henderson, N. Moonlife 2069
At the Saturday Matinee. Bradley, V.
Atherton, Marguerite. Old King Cole's Christmas. In Kamerman, S.
        A Treasury of Christmas Plays. 11+ char
AUSTRIA
        Crichton, M. Silent Night
Author of Liberty. Hark, M. and McQueen, N.
AUTOMOBILES
        Murray, J. The Driving Lesson
        _____. The Highway Restaurant
AUTUMN
        Gilfond, H. The Last Leaf

- B -

Baba Yaga. Mahlmann, L.
BABIES
        Mahlmann, L. Rumpelstiltskin
BABYSITTERS
        Bradley, V. The Big Red Heart
Bag of Gold. Korty, C.
BAGHDAD
        Winther, B. Abu Nuwas
Bailey, Anne Howard. The Christmas Visitor. In Kamerman, S.
        A Treasury of Christmas Plays. 9+ char; in Kamerman, S.
        On Stage for Christmas.
Barbee, Lindsay. The Boston Tea Party. In Kamerman, S. Patri-
        otic and Historical Plays for Young People. 7 char
        _____. A Guide for George Washington. In Kamerman,
        S. Patriotic and Historical Plays for Young People. 6 char
Bargain Day. Murray, J.
Barr, June. A White Christmas. In Kamerman, S. A Treasury of
        Christmas Plays. 5+ char
BASEBALL
        Harris, A. Yankee Doodle Dandies
        Henderson, N. Casey at the Bat
BASKETBALL
        Bradley, V. Abe Lincoln: Star Center
Bata's Lessons. Winther, B.
Bauman, A. F. Close Encounter of a Weird Kind. In Kamerman, S.
        Space and Science Fiction Plays for Young People. 8 char

_____. Santa's Alphabet. In Kamerman, S. On Stage for
Christmas. 29 char
BEAUTY
      Mahlmann, L. Beauty and the Beast
          _____. Cinderella
          _____. Rapunzel's Tower
          _____. Sleeping Beauty
      Marks, B. The Beauty Potion
      Winther, B. Follow the River Lai
Beauty and the Beast. Mahlmann, L.
The Beauty Potion. Marks, B. & R.
Beck, Warren. The Estabrook Nieces. In Beck, W. Imagination,
    and Four Other One Act Plays for Boys and Girls. 8 char
    _____. False Pretenses. In Beck, W. Imagination, and 4 Other
    One Act Plays for Boys and Girls. 11 char
    _____. Great Caesar. In Beck, W. Imagination, and Four Other
    One Act Plays for Boys and Girls. 7 char
    _____. Imagination. In Beck, W. Imagination, and Four Other
    One Act Plays for Boys and Girls. 5 char
    _____. The Old Sleuth. In Beck, W. Imagination, and 4 Other
    One Act Plays for Boys and Girls. 10 char
Belling the Cat. Carlson, B.
Bennett, Rowena. Granny Goodman's Christmas. In Kamerman, S.
    A Treasury of Christmas Plays. 12+ char
    _____. Piccola. In Kamerman, S. Christmas Play Favorites for
    Young People. 5 char
    _____. Victory Ball. In Kamerman, S. Patriotic and Historical
    Plays for Young People. Unspecified
Better Luck Tomorrow, Mr. Washington. Bradley, V.
BETTING
      Gilfond, H. The Celebrated Jumping Frog of Calaveras
          County
      Rockwell, T. How to Eat Fried Worms
Beware of the Glump. Bradley, V.
Beware the Quickly Who. Nicol, E.
BIBLE
      Rembrandt, E. Amos, Man of Tekoah
          _____. Stranger in the Land
Bierce, Ambrose. Shipwreck. In Gilfond, H. Walker Plays for
    Reading. 10 char
Big Burger. Martin, J.
The Big Red Heart. Bradley, V.
BIRDS
      Carlson, B. The Law of the Jungle
      Mahlmann, L. The Blue Willow
          _____. The Elephant's Child
          _____. The Emperor's Nightingale
          _____. Manora, the Bird Princess
          _____. Snow White and Rose Red
The Birds' Christmas Carol. Wiggin, K. D.
A Birthday Anthem for America. Olfson, L.

The Birthday of the Infanta. Walker, S.
BIRTHDAYS
     Bradley, A. Paddington Has a Birthday
     Bradley, V. Miss Lacey and the President
     Chorpenning, C. The Sleeping Beauty
BLACK AMERICANS
     Donahue, J. The Cookie Jar
     Winther, B. John Henry
BLACK HISTORY WEEK
     Winther, B. John Henry
The Blacksmith and the Carpenter. McCaslin, N.
BLACKWELL, ELIZABETH
     Henderson, N. M.D. in Petticoats
BLINDNESS
     Bradley, V. Torko the Terrible
The Bling Said Hello. Guay, G.
Blown Off the Billboard. Martin, J.
The Blue Willow. Mahlmann, L.
BOASTING
     Olfson, L. The Braggart's Clever Wife
Boiko, Claire. The Book That Saved the Earth. In Kamerman, S.
     Space and Science Fiction Plays for Young People. 7 char
     _____. The Christmas Revel. In Kamerman, S. Christmas Play
     Favorites for Young People. 16+ char
     _____. Escape to the Blue Planet. In Kamerman, S. Space and
     Science Fiction Plays for Young People. 11 char
     _____. The Petticoat Revolution. In Kamerman, S. Patriotic
     and Historical Plays for Young People. 14 char
     _____. Take Me to Your Marshal. In Kamerman, S. Space
     and Science Fiction Plays for Young People. 10 char
     _____. We Interrupt This Program. In Kamerman, S. On Stage
     for Christmas. 32 char
Bolt, Carol. My Best Friend Is Twelve Feet High. In Anonymous.
     Kids' Plays. 5 char
Bonds of Affection. DuBois, Graham
The Book That Saved the Earth. Boiko, C.
BOOK WEEK
     Chaloner, G. The Bookworm
BOOKS
     Boiko, C. The Book That Saved the Earth
     Chaloner, G. The Bookworm
     Winther, B. Follow the River Lai
The Bookworm. Chaloner, G.
BOOKWORMS
     Chaloner, G. The Bookworm
Boshibari and the Two Thieves. Nolan, P. T.
The Boston Tea Party. Barbee, L.
The Boston Tea Party. Ross, L.
BOSTON TEA PARTY
     Boiko, C. The Petticoat Revolution
     Ross, L. The Boston Tea Party

The Boy, Abe. Smith, B.
BOY SCOUTS
    Crew, H. The Password
The Bracelet Engagement. Bradley, V.
Bradley, Alfred. The Arrival of Paddington. In Bradley, A. and
    M. Bond. Paddington on Stage. 7 char
    _____. Paddington Goes to the Hospital. In Bradley, A. and
    Michael Bond. Paddington on Stage. 7 char
    _____. Paddington Goes to the Launderette. In Bradley, A.
    and Bond, M. Paddington on Stage. 5 char
    _____. Paddington Has a Birthday. In Bradley, A. and Bond,
    M. Paddington on Stage. 8 char
    _____. Paddington Paints a Picture. In Bradley, A. and Bond,
    M. Paddington on Stage. 8 char
    _____. Paddington Turns Detective. In Bradley, A. and Bond,
    M. Paddington on Stage. 9 char
    _____. Paddington Visits the Dentist. In Bradley, A. and Bond,
    M. Paddington on Stage. 8 char
Bradley, Virginia. Abe Lincoln: Star Center. In Bradley, V.
    Holidays on Stage: A Festival of Special-Occasion Plays.
    10+ char
    _____. Amateur Night at Cucumber Center. In Bradley, V. Is
    There an Actor in the House? 9+ char
    _____. Apples for Sale. In Bradley, V. Is There an Actor in
    the House? 4 char
    _____. Arizona Pilgrims. In Bradley, V. Holidays on Stage:
    A Festival of Special-Occasion Plays. 7 char
    _____. At the Saturday Matinee. In Bradley, V. At the Satur-
    day Matinee. 10+ char
    _____. Better Luck Tomorrow, Mr. Washington. In Bradley, V.
    Is There an Actor in the House? 3 char+
    _____. Beware of the Glump. In Bradley, V. Is There an Actor
    in the House? 7+ char
    _____. The Big Red Heart. In Bradley, V. Holidays on Stage:
    A Festival of Special-Occasion Plays. 6 char
    _____. The Bracelet Engagement. In Bradley, V. Stage Eight;
    One Act Plays. 6 char
    _____. Callyope, the Crying Comic. In Bradley, V. Is There
    an Actor in the House? 8 char
    _____. The Carousel and a Cold Fried Egg. In Bradley, V.
    Stage Eight; One Act Plays. 10+ char
    _____. Don't Fall Asleep, Coach, You Might Possibly Dream. In
    Bradley, V. Is There an Actor in the House? 9 char
    _____. Five Times Sue Is Julia Bates. In Bradley, V. Stage
    Eight; One Act Plays. 6 char
    _____. Flat, Flat, Flat. In Bradley, V. Is There an Actor in
    the House? 11 char
    _____. The Greater Miracle. In Bradley, V. Holidays on Stage:
    A Festival of Special-Occasion Plays. 4 char
    _____. A Groundhog by Any Other Name. In Bradley, V. Holi-
    days on Stage: A Festival of Special-Occasion Plays. 5+ char

_____. Gwendolyn Gloria Gertrude McFee. In Bradley, V. Is There an Actor in the House? 19 char

_____. The Haunted House. In Bradley, V. Is There an Actor in the House? 9+ char

_____. Help! In Bradley, V. Is There an Actor in the House? 7+ char

_____. Here Lies McClean. In Bradley, V. Is There an Actor in the House? 7 char

_____. Herlock Sholmes. In Bradley, V. Is There an Actor in the House? 9 char

_____. Hibernian Picnic. In Bradley, V. Is There an Actor in the House? 8+ char

_____. How Did We Manage Before the Postman Came? In Bradley, V. Is There an Actor in the House? 12 char

_____. If the Rabbit Pickets, You're Doing Something Wrong. In Bradley, V. Is There an Actor in the House? 7+ char

_____. If You Recognize Me, Don't Admit It. In Bradley, V. Is There an Actor in the House? 20+ char

_____. The Last Bus from Lockerbee. In Bradley, V. Stage Eight; One Act Plays. 9+ char

_____. Ludlillian and the Dark Road. In Bradley, V. Holidays on Stage: A Festival of Special-Occasion Plays. 7+ char

_____. Miss Lacey and the President. In Bradley, V. Holidays on Stage: A Festival of Special-Occasion Plays. 8 char

_____. Mrs. Clopsaddle Presents Christmas. In Bradley, V. Is There an Actor in the House? 7 char

_____. Mrs. Clopsaddle Presents Spring. In Bradley, V. Is There an Actor in the House? 12 char

_____. Nester the Jester. In Bradley, V. Is There an Actor in the House? 10 char

_____. The Night That Time Sat Still. In Bradley, V. Holidays on Stage: A Festival of Special-Occasion Plays. 10 char

_____. None but the Strong. In Bradley, V. Is There an Actor in the House? 3 char+

_____. Nothing Will Rattle a Regnant Soul. In Bradley, V. Stage Eight: One Act Plays. 8+ char

_____. Off Guard. In Bradley, V. Holidays on Stage: A Festival of Special-Occasion Plays. 5 char

_____. Quick! The River's Rising. In Bradley, V. Is There an Actor in the House? 8 char

_____. Repeat After Me. In Bradley, V. Is There an Actor in the House? 9 char

_____. A Roll of Nickels. In Bradley, V. Stage Eight; One Act Plays. 8+ char

_____. Shoes and Ships and a Mermaid. In Bradley, V. Is There an Actor in the House? 9 char

_____. The Story of John Worthington Snee. In Bradley, V. Is There an Actor in the House? 17+ char

_____. Sunday at Meadowlake Manor. In Bradley, V. Is There an Actor in the House? 10+ char

_____. Surprise. In Bradley, V. Is There an Actor in the House? 5+ char

_____. Tillie's Terror. In Bradley, V. Is There an Actor in the House? 6 char

_____. Torko the Terrible. In Bradley, V. Is There an Actor in the House? 16+ char

_____. Turkeys Take a Dim View of Thanksgiving. In Bradley, V. Is There an Actor in the House? 5 char

_____. Walk-Up on Christopher. In Bradley, V. Stage Eight; One Act Plays. 6 char

_____. What Counts at the County Fair. In Bradley, V. Is There an Actor in the House? 3 char

_____. What Took You So Long? In Bradley, V. Is There an Actor in the House? 9+ char

_____. What Will You Tell Us of Christmas? In Bradley, V. Holidays on Stage: A Festival of Special-Occasion Plays. 7+ char

_____. Women's Lib Comes to the Hill Country. In Bradley, V. Is There an Actor in the House? 4 char

_____. You Can't Blame Women for Coming Out of the Kitchen. In Bradley, V. Is There an Actor in the House? 4 char

_____. You Can't Win 'Em All. In Bradley, V. Is There an Actor in the House? 4 char

_____. You Have to Stay on the Horse. In Bradley, V. Stage Eight; One Act Plays. 6 char

The Braggart's Clever Wife. Olfson, L.

BRAVERY
     Miller, H. Mr. Snow White's Thanksgiving
     Olfson, L. The Braggart's Clever Wife

The Broomstick Beauty. Miller, H.

BROTHERHOOD
     Dias, E. Christmas Spirit
     Donahue, J. Old Kieg of Malfi
     DuBois, G. A Room for a King
     Runnette, H. The Way
     Waite, H. The Master of the Strait

Brown, Abbie. The Lantern. In Brown, A. The Lantern, and Other Plays for Children. 13+ char

_____. The Little Shadows. In Brown, A. F. The Lantern, and Other Plays for Children. 5 char

_____. Rhoecus. In Brown, A. F. The Lantern, and Other Plays for Children. 4 char

_____. The Wishing Moon. In Brown, A. The Lantern, and Other Plays for Children. 19 char

Brown, Carol. The Constitution Is Born. In Kamerman, S. Patriotic and Historical Plays for Young People. 14 char

BUDDHA
     Winther, B. Pacca, the Little Bowman

The Buffalo and the Bell. Wheetley, K.

Building the House. Korty, C.

The Building and the Statue. Martin, J.

BUILDINGS
     Martin, J. The Building and the Statue

Bumbo and Scrumbo and Blinko. Jagendorf, M.
BUNKER HILL
    Boiko, C. The Petticoat Revolution
Bunnies and Bonnets. McGowan, J.
BURMA
    Winther, B. White Elephant
BUTTERFLIES
    Martin, J. Hands Off! Don't Touch!

- C -

CAESAR, JULIUS
    Beck, W. Great Caesar
CALAMITY JANE
    Deary, T. The Custard Kid
Callanan, Cecelia. Cupid and Company. In Kamerman, S. Holiday
    Plays Around the Year. 4 char
Callyope, the Crying Comic. Bradley, V.
Campbell, Paddy. Chinook. In Anonymous. Kids' Plays. 6 char
Candles for Christmas. Howard, Helen L.
Capell, Loretta Camp. The First Christmas Tree. In Kamerman, S.
    A Treasury of Christmas Plays. 5+ char
CAREERS
    Bradley, V. Gwendolyn Gloria Gertrude McFee
    _____. The Story of John Worthington Snee
    _____. Walk-Up on Christopher
Carlson, Bernice. Anyone Could, but--. In Carlson, B. Let's Find
    the Big Idea. 9 char
_____. Belling the Cat. In Carlson, B. Let's Find the Big Idea.
    7+ char
_____. Clever--Eh? In Carlson, B. Let's Find the Big Idea.
    6 char
_____. The Country Mouse and the City Mouse. In Carlson, B.
    Let's Find the Big Idea. 5 char
_____. Crowded? In Carlson, B. Let's Find the Big Idea. 7
    char
_____. Half of the Reward. In Carlson, B. Let's Find the Big
    Idea. 7 char
_____. The Heart of a Monkey. In Carlson, B. Let's Find the
    Big Idea. 2 char
_____. The Law of the Jungle. In Carlson, B. Let's Find the
    Big Idea. 15 char
_____. Lion, Sick and Dying. In Carlson, B. Let's Find the Big
    Idea. 6 char
_____. A Pearl in the Barnyard. In Carlson, B. Let's Find the
    Big Idea. 6+ char
_____. Problems! Problems! In Carlson, B. Let's Find the Big
    Idea. 9 char
_____. Rain or Shine. In Carlson, B. Let's Find the Big Idea.
    5 char

_____. So Proud. In Carlson, B. W. Let's Find the Big Idea.
4 char

_____. Think Twice. In Carlson, B. Let's Find the Big Idea.
3 char

_____. The Tiger, the Brahman, and the Jackal. In Carlson,
B. Let's Find the Big Idea. 9+ char

_____. Together or Alone? In Carlson, B. Let's Find the Big
Idea. 8 char

_____. Who Would Steal a Penny? In Carlson, B. Let's Find
the Big Idea. 9 char

_____. The Whole Truth. In Carlson, B. Let's Find the Big
Idea. 5 char

_____. Who's Stronger? In Carlson, B. Let's Find the Big
Idea. 3 char

The Carousel and a Cold Fried Egg. Bradley, V.

A Case for Two Detectives. Murray, J.

The Case of the Kidnapped Nephew. Alexander, S.

Casey at the Bat. Thayer, E.

The Cask of Amontillado. Poe, E. A.

CASTLES
     Watkins, M. Nobody Believes in Witches

Catastrophe Clarence. Shore, M.

CATS
     Alexander, S. Meow! and Arf!
     Carlson, B. Belling the Cat
     _____. The Country Mouse and the City Mouse
     Christmas, J. Three Little Kittens' Christmas
     DeRegniers, B. The Magic Spell
     Lynch-Watson, J. The Little Red Hen
     Mahlmann, L. The Blue Willow
     _____. King Midas and the Golden Touch
     _____. Perez and Martina
     _____. Puss in Boots
     McCaslin, N. The Talking Cat
     Rockwell, T. Myron Mere

Cavanah, Frances. Mr. Bunny's Prize. In Jagendorf, M. One-Act
Plays for Young Folks. 11 char

_____. The Transfiguration of the Gifts. In McSweeny, M.
Christmas Plays for Young Players. 9+ char

The Celebrated Jumping Frog of Calareras County. Twain, M.

Chaloner, Gwen. The Bookworm. In Kamerman, S. Holiday Plays
Around the Year. 8 char

CHANUKAH
     Bradley, V. The Greater Miracle
     Gabriel, M. Chanukah Story
     Rembrandt, E. The Sacrifice

Chanukah Story. Gabriel, M.

Chekhov, A. The Upheaval. In Gilfond, H. Walker Plays for Reading. 6 char

Chermak, Sylvia. The Elves and the Shoemaker. In Kamerman, S.
Christmas Play Favorites for Young People. 2+ char

The Chicken and the Egg. Martin, J.
CHILDREN
      Mahlmann, L. The Pied Piper of Hamelin
CHINA
      Harris, A. Ming Lee and the Magic Tree
      Mahlmann, L. The Blue Willow
      _____. The Emperor's Nightingale
      Nolan, P. The Double Nine of Chih Yuan
      Winther, B. Ah Wing Fu and the Golden Dragon
CHINESE NEW YEAR
      Henderson, N. Hail the Lucky Year
Chinook. Campbell, P.
CHORAL PLAYS
      Bennett, R. Victory Ball
      Bradley, V. What Will You Tell Us of Christmas?
      Fisher, A. George Washington, Farmer
      _____. Sing, America, Sing
      _____. Sing the Songs of Christmas
      _____. Washington Marches On
      Kamerman, S. Nine Cheers for Christmas
      McGowan, J. The Coming of the Prince
      Oberacker, S. A Christmas Tale
      Olfson, L. A Birthday Anthem for America
      _____. Sing a Song of Holidays!
      Traditional. A Christmas Pageant
Chorpenning, Charlotte. The Sleeping Beauty. In Jennings, C.
   and A. Harris. Plays Children Love. 12 char
The Chosen One. Duvall, L.
CHRISTMAS
      Albert, R. A New Angle on Christmas
      Alexander, S. Tricky Gifts
      Atherton, M. Old King Cole's Christmas
      Bailey, A. The Christmas Visitor
      Barbee, L. A Guide for George Washington
      Barr, J. A White Christmas
      Bauman, A. Santa's Alphabet
      Bennett, R. Granny Goodman's Christmas
      _____. Piccola
      Boiko, C. The Christmas Revel
      _____. We Interrupt This Program...
      Bradley, V. The Last Bus from Lockerbee
      _____. Mrs. Clopsaddle Presents Christmas
      _____. What Will You Tell Us of Christmas?
      Brown, A. The Little Shadows
      Capell, L. The First Christmas Tree
      Carlson, B. The Country Mouse and the City Mouse
      Cavanah, F. The Transfiguration of the Gifts
      Chernak, S. A Visit from St. Nicholas
      Christmas, J. Three Little Kittens' Christmas
      Clapp, P. Christmas in Old New England
      Crichton, M. Silent Night

Dias, E. Christmas Spirit
_____. The Christmas Starlet
DuBois, G. The Humblest Place
_____. A Room for a King
_____. Star Over Bethlehem
Duvall, L. The Chosen One
_____. Little Chip's Christmas Tree
Fawcett, M. The Talking Christmas Tree
Fisher, A. Mr. Scrooge Finds Christmas
_____. Sing the Songs of Christmas
_____. Up a Christmas Tree
Gaines, F. A Christmas Carol
Hackett, W. Incident at Valley Forge
_____. A Merry Christmas
Hark, M. Christmas Recaptured
_____. Christmas Shopping Early
_____. Merry Christmas, Crawfords!
_____. Merry Christmas Customs
_____. Reindeer on the Roof
_____. What, No Santa Claus?
Head, F. The Second Shepherd's Play
Henderson, N. Keeping Christmas Merry
Holbrook, M. The Toymaker's Doll
Hoppenstedt, E. Santa Goes Mod
Howard, H. Candles for Christmas
Jensen, S. North Pole Confidential
Kamerman, S. Nine Cheers for Christmas
Korty, C. The Year Santa Forgot Christmas
Leuser, E. The Christmas Sampler
_____. The Legend of the Christmas Rose
Mahlmann, L. The Nutcracker Prince
Majeski, B. Whatever Happened to Good Old Ebenezer
      Scrooge?
Martens, A. Santa Claus Is Twins
_____. Star of Bethlehem
_____. Visions of Sugar Plums
McGowan, J. Christmas Every Day
_____. The Coming of the Prince
_____. Santa Claus for President
_____. The Santa Claus Twins
McSweeny, M. The Christmas Party
_____. Listen to the Peace and Goodwill
_____. Santa! Please Get Up
Miller, H. The Birds' Christmas Carol
_____. A Christmas Promise
_____. The Left-Over Reindeer
_____. Monsieur Santa Claus
_____. Puppy Love
_____. Red Carpet Christmas
_____. Season's Greetings
Mills, G. Christmas Comes to Hamelin

Moessenger, B. Man in the Red Suit
Moessinger, W. He Won't Be Home for Christmas
Morley, O. Little Women
_____. O Little Town of Bethlehem
Murray, J. The Greatest Christmas Gift
Newman, D. The Christmas Question
Nicholson, J. Holiday for Santa
Nolan, P. And Christmas Is Its Name
_____. The Trouble with Christmas
Oberacker, S. A Christmas Tale
Olfson, L. The Bird's Christmas Carol
_____. A Christmas Carol
_____. Christmas Coast to Coast
_____. Nine Times Christmas
Owen, D. The Green Stone
_____. In Search of Christmas
Patterson, E. No Room at the Inn
Peacock, M. Keeping Christmas
Pendleton, E. 'Twas the Night Before Christmas
Peterson, M. Adobe Christmas
Phillips, M. Violets for Christmas
Runnette, H. Touchstone
_____. The Way
Spamer, C. Twinkle
Sroda, A. Santa Changes His Mind
Thane, A. A Christmas Carol
_____. Christmas Every Day
_____. The Christmas Nutcracker
Thurston, M. Room for Mary
Traditional. A Christmas Pageant
Urban, C. Mrs. Claus' Christmas Present
Very, A. The Shoemaker and the Elves
Waite, H. The Master of the Strait
Wilson, E. The Least of These
Winther, B. The Villain and the Toy Shop
Wright, D. The Twelve Days of Christmas
Christmas at the O.K. Corral. Miller, P. and Thurston, C.
A Christmas Carol. Dickens, C.
A Christmas Carol. Dickens, C. (Play title: Mr. Scrooge Finds
    Christmas, Written by Fisher, A.)
CHRISTMAS CAROLS
    Olfson, L. The Bird's Christmas Carol
Christmas Coast to Coast. Olfson, L.
Christmas Comes to Hamelin. Mills, G.
CHRISTMAS CUSTOMS
    Runnette, H. The Way
Christmas Every Day. Howells, W. D.
Christmas in Old New England. Clapp, P.
CHRISTMAS IN OTHER COUNTRIES
    Nolan, P. And Christmas Is Its Name
Christmas, Joyce. Three Little Kittens' Christmas. In Kamerman,
    S. On Stage for Christmas. 11 char

The Christmas Nutcracker. Thane, A.
A Christmas Pageant. Traditional
The Christmas Party. McSweeny, M.
A Christmas Promise. Miller, H.
The Christmas Question. Newman, D.
Christmas Recaptured. Hark, M. and McQueen, N.
The Christmas Revel. Boiko, C.
The Christmas Sampler. Leuser, E.
Christmas Shopping Early. Hark, M. and McQueen, N.
Christmas Spirit. Dias, E.
The Christmas Starlet. Dias, E.
A Christmas Tale. Oberacker, S.
CHRISTMAS TREES
  Bailey, A. The Christmas Visitor
  Capell, L. The First Christmas Tree
  Fawcett, M. The Talking Christmas Tree
  Fisher, A. Up a Christmas Tree
  Hark, M. Merry Christmas, Crawfords!
The Christmas Visitor. Bailey, A.
Cinderella. Mahlmann, L.
CIRCUS
  Bradley, V. Callyope, the Crying Comic
  Donahue, J. How Could You Tell
CIVIL RIGHTS
  Henderson, N. Soul Force
CIVIL WAR
  DuBois, G. Bonds of Affection
  Grinins, T. To Test the Truth
  Henderson, N. Keeping Christmas Merry
  Miller, H. Old Glory Grows Up
Clapp, Patricia. Christmas in Old New England. In Kamerman, S.
  Holiday Plays Around the Year. 6 char
Clever Clyde. Korty, C.
Clever--Eh? Carlson, B.
CLEVERNESS
  Carlson, B. Clever--Eh?
  Mahlmann, L. Aesop's Fables
  _____. Puss in Boots
  _____. The Three Little Pigs
  Winther, B. Abu Nuwas
  _____. Listen to the Hodja
  _____. Little Mouse-Deer
Close Encounter of a Weird Kind. Bauman, A.
CLOWNS
  Alexander, S. Tricky Gifts
  Korty, C. Bag of Gold
  _____. Building the House
  _____. Clever Clyde
  _____. The Flagpole
  _____. Opera Singer
  _____. The Pumpkin

_____. The Road to Market
_____. Stretch the Bench
Marks, B. The Concert
_____. The Rope
CLUBS (ASSOCIATIONS)
    Carlson, B. Who Would Steal a Penny?
CODES
    Bradley, V. Surprise
COINS
    Carlson, B. Who Would Steal a Penny?
Collodi, Carlo. Pinocchio and the Fire-Eater. In Jennings, C.
    and A. Harris. Plays Children Love. 16+ char
COLUMBUS, CHRISTOPHER
    Priore, F. 1492 Blues
COLUMBUS DAY
    Priore, F. 1492 Blues
Come Quick! Alexander, S.
Come to the Fair. Henderson, N.
COMEDY
    Boiko, C. The Petticoat Revolution
    Callanan, C. Cupid and Company
    Creative Dramatics. Robots for Sale
    Dias, E. Horse Sense
    Fontaine, R. Next Stop, Saturn
    Grinins, T. To Test the Truth
    Harris, A. A Toby Show
    Lane, M. Is There Life on Other Planets?
    Murray, J. Visitor from Outer Space
    Priore, F. 1492 Blues
    Willment, F. The Whites of Their Eyes
Comfort, Florence C. The Sing-a-Song Man. In Jagendorf, M.
    One-Act Plays for Young Folks. 6+ char
The Coming of the Prince. McGowan, J.
COMMUNICATION
    Bradley, V. How Did We Manage Before the Postman Came?
COMPUTERS
    Gabriel, M. The Holiday Machine
    Hark, M. Christmas Shopping Early
    Murray, J. Home Sweet Home Computer
The Concert. Marks, B. & R.
CONSTITUTION
    Brown, C. The Constitution Is Born
    Fisher, A. When Freedom Was News
The Constitution Is Born. Brown, C.
CONTESTS
    Bradley, V. What Counts at the County Fair
    Hark, M. Reindeer on the Roof
    Owen, D. Hooray for the Cup
The Cookie Jar. Donahue, J.
COOKING
    Fisher, A. A Dish of Green Peas

Lawler, L. In the Kitchen of the King
Marks, B. The Cooking Lesson
McSweeny, M. Santa! Please Get Up
The Cooking Lesson. Marks, B. & R.
The Copetown City Kite Crisis. Deverell, R.
The Country Mouse and the City Mouse. Carlson, B.
COURAGE
    Barbee, L. A Guide for George Washington
    Bradley, V. None but the Strong
    Fisher, A. "Molly Pitcher"
    Golden, J. Johnny Moonbeam and the Silver Arrow
    Hackett, W. Incident at Valley Forge
    Hall, M. Molly Pitcher Meets the General
    Harris, A. Steal Away Home
    _____. Yankee Doodle Dandies
    Kane, E. Paul Revere of Boston
    Mahlmann, L. The Little Indian Brave
    _____. Manora, the Bird Princess
    Mason, T. Robin Hood: A Story of the Forest
    Nolan, P. The Gates of Dinkelsbuehl
    _____. A Leak in the Dike
    _____. The Son of William Tell
    _____. The Trial of Peter Zenger
    Phillips, M. All Because of a Scullery Maid
    Smith, J. Summer Soldier
The Courters. Nolan, P.
COWBOYS
    Bradley, V. The Story of John Worthington Snee
    Fisher, A. Sing, America, Sing
Creative Dramatics. Robots for Sale. In Kamerman, S. Space and
    Science Fiction Plays for Young People. 7+ char
Crew, Helen. The Password. In Jagendorf, M. One-Act Plays for
    Young People. 15+ char
Crichton, Madge. Silent Night. In Kamerman, S. On Stage for
    Christmas. 7 char
Crowded? Carlson, B.
CRUSADES
    Mason, T. Robin Hood: A Story of the Forest
CUB SCOUTS
    Murray, J. Den Mother
Cupid and Company. Callanan, C.
The Custard Kid. Deary, T.

- D -

DANCING
    Bradley, V. Amateur Night at Cucumber Center
    _____. Hibernian Picnic
    _____. Mrs. Clopsaddle Presents Spring
    Henderson, N. Come to the Fair

Mahlmann, L. The Nutcracker Prince
_____. Perez and Martina
Maloney, L. I Didn't Know That!
Miller, H. A Christmas Promise
Nolan, P. The Highland Fling
Winther, B. Ah Wing Fu and the Golden Dragon
_____. Little Mouse-Deer
_____. White Elephant
David Swan. Gilfond, H.
Dead of Night. Murray, J.
Deary, Terence. Adventure Island. In Deary, T. Teaching
Through Theatre: 6 Practical Projects. 4 char
_____. The Custard Kid. In Deary, T. Teaching Through
Theatre: 6 Practical Projects. 4 char
_____. The Factory. In Deary, T. Teaching Through Theatre:
6 Practical Projects. 5 char
_____. Glorygum. In Deary, T. Teaching Through Theatre:
6 Practical Projects. 4 char
_____. The King of Tarantulus. In Deary, T. Teaching
Through Theatre: 6 Practical Projects. 4 char
_____. Super Village. In Deary, T. Teaching Through Theatre:
6 Practical Projects. 9 char
DEATH
Carlson, B. Lion, Sick and Dying
Gilfond, H. The Duel
_____. The Last Leaf
Mahlmann, L. The Emperor's Nightingale
Murray, J. The Door
Nolan, P. The Magic of Salamanca
Rembrandt, E. So Young to Die
Shaw, R. Sleeping Beauty
Traditional. Punch and Judy
Warren, L. The Palmwine Drinkard
Winther, B. Bata's Lessons
DECLARATION OF INDEPENDENCE
Fisher, A. Ask Mr. Jefferson
_____. Our Great Declaration
_____. A Star for Old Glory
Hark, M. Author of Liberty
Slingluff, M. Naughty Susan
Wolman, D. An Imaginary Trial of George Washington
deMaupassant, Guy. The Necklace. In Gilfond, H. Walker Plays
for Reading. 4 char
DEMOCRACY
Nolan, P. The Skill of Pericles
Wolman, D. An Imaginary Trial of George Washington
Den Mother. Murray, J.
DeRegniers, Beatrice Schenk. The Magic Spell. In DeRegniers, B.
Picture Book Theater. 5 char
_____. The Mysterious Stranger. In DeRegniers, B. Picture
Book Theater. 8 char

DETECTIVES
      Alexander, S.　The Case of the Kidnapped Nephew
      _____.　Mystery of the Stone Statues
      _____.　Whatever Happened to Uncle Albert?
      Bradley, V.　Herlock Sholmes
      Murray, J.　A Case for Two Detectives
      _____.　I Want to Report a Murder
Deverell, Rex.　The Copetown City Kite Crisis.　In Anonymous.
    Kids Plays.　7 char
DEVIL
      Harris, A.　Punch and Judy
      Traditional.　Punch and Judy
      Winther, B.　Japanese Trio
Dias, Earl J.　Christmas Spirit.　In Kamerman, S.　Christmas Play
    Favorites for Young People.　8 char
_____.　Christmas Spirit.　In Kamerman, S.　A Treasury of
    Christmas Plays.　8 char
_____.　The Christmas Starlet.　In Kamerman, S.　On Stage for
    Christmas.　11 char
_____.　Horse Sense.　In Kamerman, S.　Patriotic and Historical
    Plays for Young People.　7 char
_____.　The Little Man Who Wasn't There.　In Kamerman, S.
    Space and Science Fiction Plays for Young People.　7 char
_____.　Martha Washington's Spy.　In Kamerman, S.　Patriotic
    and Historical Plays for Young People.　7 char
Dickens, Charles.　A Christmas Carol (Play title:　Mr. Scrooge Finds
    Christmas, written by Fisher, A.)
_____.　A Christmas Carol.　In Kamerman, S.　On Stage for
    Christmas.　24 char
_____.　A Christmas Carol.　In Kamerman, S.　A Treasury of
    Christmas Plays.　16 char
_____.　Mr. Scrooge Finds Christmas.　In Kamerman, S.　Christ-
    mas Play Favorites for Young People.　18+ char
DIET
      Murray, J.　Do or Diet
A Dish of Green Peas.　Fisher, A.
Do or Diet.　Murray, J.
DOCTORS
      Comfort, F.　The Sing-a-Song Man
      Henderson, N.　M.D. in Petticoats
      Traditional.　Punch and Judy
DOGS
      Alexander, S.　Meow! and Arf!
      Mahlmann, L.　The Blue Willow
      Marra, D.　"Woof" for the Red, White and Blue
      Miller, H.　Puppy Love
DOLLS
      Boiko, C.　The Christmas Revel
      Holbrook, M.　The Toymaker's Doll
      Mills, G.　Christmas Comes to Hamelin
      Owen, D.　In Search of Christmas

Donahue, John. The Cookie Jar. In Donahue, J. The Cookie Jar
and Other Plays. 21 char
_____. How Could You Tell. In Donahue, J. The Cookie Jar
and Other Plays. 40 char
_____. Old Kieg of Malfi. In Donahue, J. The Cookie Jar and
Other Plays. 25+ char
Don't Fall Asleep, Coach, You Might Possibly Dream. Bradley, V.
The Door. Murray, J.
The Double Nine of Chih Yuan. Nolan, P.
The Dragon Hammer. Kraus, J.
DRAGONS
    Janney, S. The East Wind's Revenge
    Marks, B. The Beauty Potion
    Owen, D. Hooray for the Cup
    Winther, B. Ah Wing Fu and the Golden Dragon
    _____. Fire Demon and South Wind
DREAMS
    Bradley, V. Don't Fall Asleep, Coach, You Might Possibly
      Dream
    Gaines, F. A Christmas Carol
    Nolan, P. The Golden Voice of Little Erik
    O'Donnell, T. The Sandman's Brother
    Wilson, E. The Least of These
The Driving Lesson. Murray, J.
Du Bois, Graham. Bonds of Affection. In Kamerman, S. Holiday
Plays Around the Year. 6+ char
_____. The End of the Road. In Kamerman, S. Holiday Plays
Around the Year. 7 char
_____. Every Day Is Thanksgiving. In Kamerman, S. Holiday
Plays Around the Year. 9 char
_____. The Humblest Place. In Kamerman, S. A Treasury of
Christmas Plays. 11+ char
_____. A Room for a King. In Kamerman, Sylvia. A Treasury
of Christmas Plays. 10 char
_____. Star Over Bethlehem. In Kamerman, S. On Stage for
Christmas. 12+ char
The Duel. Gilfond, H.
Dumas, Alexandre. The Duel. In Gilfond, H. Walker Plays for
Reading. 10 char
Duvall, Lucille. The Chosen One. In Kamerman, S. A Treasury
of Christmas Plays. 10 char
_____. Little Chip's Christmas Tree. In Kamerman, S. A Treas-
ury of Christmas Plays. 19 char
DWARFS
    Mahlmann, L. King of the Golden River
    _____. Rumpelstiltskin
    _____. Snow White and Rose Red
    Majeski, B. Whatever Happened to Good Old Ebenezer
      Scrooge?
    White, J. Snow White and the Seven Dwarfs

- E -

ESKIMOS
    Ross, L. Where There Is No North
The Estabrook Nieces. Beck, W.
Even a Child Can Do It. Murray, J.
Everybody, Everybody. Martin, J.
Everyday Is Thanksgiving. DuBois, G.
EVIL
    Chorpenning, C. The Sleeping Beauty
    Deary, T. The King of Tarantulus
    Mahlmann, L. The Nutcracker Prince
    _____. Sleeping Beauty
    Rockwell, T. Myron Mere
    Stokes, J. Wiley and the Hairy Man
    White, J. Snow White and the Seven Dwarfs
    Winther, B. Follow the River Lai
    _____. Prince Rama
    Ross, L. Where There is No North

- F -

FABLES
    Carlson, B. Belling the Cat
    _____. The Country Mouse and the City Mouse
    _____. The Heart of a Monkey
    _____. Lion, Sick and Dying
    _____. A Pearl in the Barnyard
    _____. So Proud
    _____. Think Twice
    _____. The Tiger, the Brahman, and the Jackal
    _____. Together or Alone?
    _____. The Whole Truth
    _____. Who's Stronger?
    Harris, A. Androcles and the Lion
    Lynch-Watson, J. The Lion and the Mouse
    Mahlmann, L. Aesop's Fables
    McCaslin, N. The Pot of Gold
The Factory. Deary, T.
FAIRIES
    Brown, A. The Wishing Moon
    Chorpenning, C. The Sleeping Beauty
    Fawcett, M. The Talking Christmas Tree
    Mahlmann, L. Anansi and the Box of Stories
    _____. Sleeping Beauty
    McGowan, J. Christmas Every Day
    Purdy, N. The Heritage
FAIRS
    Bradley, V. The Carousel and a Cold Fried Egg
    _____. What Counts at the County Fair
    Garver, J. Space Suit with Roses
FAIRY TALES
    Bradley, V. Flat, Flat, Flat

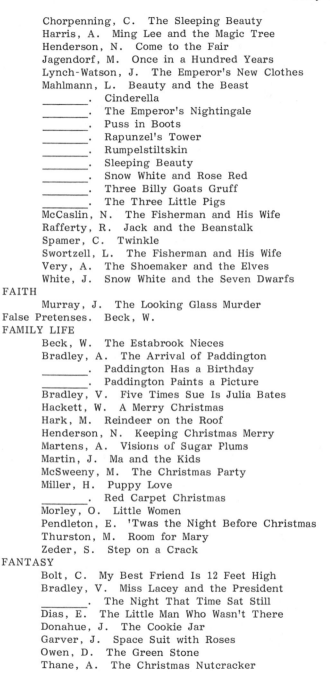

Chorpenning, C. The Sleeping Beauty
Harris, A. Ming Lee and the Magic Tree
Henderson, N. Come to the Fair
Jagendorf, M. Once in a Hundred Years
Lynch-Watson, J. The Emperor's New Clothes
Mahlmann, L. Beauty and the Beast
_____. Cinderella
_____. The Emperor's Nightingale
_____. Puss in Boots
_____. Rapunzel's Tower
_____. Rumpelstiltskin
_____. Sleeping Beauty
_____. Snow White and Rose Red
_____. Three Billy Goats Gruff
_____. The Three Little Pigs
McCaslin, N. The Fisherman and His Wife
Rafferty, R. Jack and the Beanstalk
Spamer, C. Twinkle
Swortzell, L. The Fisherman and His Wife
Very, A. The Shoemaker and the Elves
White, J. Snow White and the Seven Dwarfs
FAITH
Murray, J. The Looking Glass Murder
False Pretenses. Beck, W.
FAMILY LIFE
Beck, W. The Estabrook Nieces
Bradley, A. The Arrival of Paddington
_____. Paddington Has a Birthday
_____. Paddington Paints a Picture
Bradley, V. Five Times Sue Is Julia Bates
Hackett, W. A Merry Christmas
Hark, M. Reindeer on the Roof
Henderson, N. Keeping Christmas Merry
Martens, A. Visions of Sugar Plums
Martin, J. Ma and the Kids
McSweeny, M. The Christmas Party
Miller, H. Puppy Love
_____. Red Carpet Christmas
Morley, O. Little Women
Pendleton, E. 'Twas the Night Before Christmas
Thurston, M. Room for Mary
Zeder, S. Step on a Crack
FANTASY
Bolt, C. My Best Friend Is 12 Feet High
Bradley, V. Miss Lacey and the President
_____. The Night That Time Sat Still
Dias, E. The Little Man Who Wasn't There
Donahue, J. The Cookie Jar
Garver, J. Space Suit with Roses
Owen, D. The Green Stone
Thane, A. The Christmas Nutcracker

Zeder, S.   Step on a Crack
FARCES
    Harris, A.   Peck's Bad Boy
    Nolan, P.   Boshibari and the Two Thieves
    _____.   The French Cabinetmaker
FARMERS
    Carlson, B.   Crowded?
    _____.   Together or Alone?
    Fisher, A.   George Washington, Farmer
    Korty, C.   The Turtle Who Wanted to Fly
    Mahlmann, L.   Tale of Peter Rabbit
    McCaslin, N.   The Pot of Gold
    McSweeny, M.   The Christmas Party
    Rafferty, R.   Jack and the Beanstalk
    Wheetley, K.   The Buffalo and the Bell
    Winther, B.   Abu Nuwas
FARMS
    Carlson, B.   A Pearl in the Barnyard
Farrar, John.   The Garden at the Zoo.   In Jagendorf, M.   One-
    Act Plays for Young Folks.   15 char
FATE
    Bradley, V.   Apples for Sale
    Warren, L.   Woyenji
FATHERS
    Walker, S.   The Birthday of the Infanta
Fawcett, Margaret Georgia.   The Talking Christmas Tree.   In
    Kamerman, S.   A Treasury of Christmas Plays.   7 char
FEAR
    Bradley, V.   Beware of the Glump
    Carlson, B.   The Country Mouse and the City Mouse
    Gaines, F.   The Legend of Sleepy Hollow
FEMINISM
    Boiko, C.   The Petticoat Revolution
    Bradley, V.   Gwendolyn Gloria Gertrude McFee
    _____.   Women's Lib Comes to the Hill Country
    _____.   You Can't Blame Women for Coming Out of the
      Kitchen
    Garver, J.   Space Suit with Roses
    Henderson, N.   M.D. in Petticoats
FEUDS
    Miller, H.   Red Carpet Christmas
    Van Horn, B.   The Hillbillies and the Robots
Field, Anna and Ella Wilson.   The Least of These.   In McSweeny,
    M.   Christmas Plays for Young Players.   8+ char
Field, Eugene.   The Coming of the Prince.   In Kamerman, S.   A
    Treasury of Christmas Plays.   28+ char
The Final Curtain.   Murray, J.
Fire Demon and South Wind.   Winther, B.
The First Christmas Tree.   Capell, L.
First Day at School.   Murray, J.
FISH
    Mahlmann, L.   Manora, the Bird Princess

McCaslin, N. The Fisherman and His Wife
Swortzell, L. The Fisherman and His Wife
The Fish Story. Murray, J.
Fisher, Aileen. Ask Mr. Jefferson. In Fisher, A. Bicentennial
Plays and Programs. 5 char
_____. A Dish of Green Peas. In Fisher, A. Bicentennial Plays
and Programs. 5 char
_____. George Washington, Farmer. In Kamerman, S. Patriotic
and Historical Plays for Young People. 4+ char
_____. Our Great Declaration. In Fisher, A. Bicentennial Plays
and Programs. 20+ char
_____. "Molly Pitcher." In Fisher, A. Bicentennial Plays and
Programs. 4 char
_____. Sing, America, Sing. In Fisher, A. Bicentennial Plays
and Programs. 12+ char
_____. Sing the Songs of Christmas. In Kamerman, S. A
Treasury of Christmas Plays. 44 char
_____. Sing the Songs of Thanksgiving. In Kamerman, S.
Holiday Plays Around the Year. 11+ char
_____. A Star for Old Glory. In Fisher, A. Bicentennial Plays
and Programs. 7 char
_____. Up a Christmas Tree. In Kamerman, S. On Stage for
Christmas. 6 char
_____. Washington Marches On. In Fisher, A. Bicentennial
Plays and Programs. 33 char
_____. When Freedom Was News. In Fisher, A. Bicentennial
Plays and Programs. 10 char
_____. Yankee Doodle Dandy. In Fisher, A. Bicentennial Plays
and Programs. 8+ char
The Fisherman and His Wife. McCaslin, N.
The Fisherman and His Wife. Swortzell, L.
FISHING
Murray, J. The Fish Story
Five Ghosts. Wright, R.
Five Times Sue Is Julia Bates. Bradley, V.
The Flagpole. Korty, C.
FLAGS
Fisher, A. A Star for Old Glory
Korty, C. The Flagpole
Marra, D. "Woof" for the Red, White and Blue
FLAGS--UNITED STATES
Fisher, A. Sing, America, Sing
Miller, H. Old Glory Grows Up
Flat, Flat, Flat. Bradley, V.
Flight International. Murray, J.
FLOODS
Bradley, V. Quick! The River's Rising
FLOWERS
Martin, J. Hands Off! Don't Touch!
Shaw, R. Sleeping Beauty
The Flying Horse Machine. Winther, B.

FOLK TALES

Harris, A. Yankee Doodle Dandies
Korty, C. Ananse's Trick Does Double Work
_____. The Man Who Loved to Laugh
_____. Mr. Hare Takes Mr. Leopard for a Ride
_____. The Turtle Who Wanted to Fly
Kraus, J. The Dragon Hammer
_____. The Tale of Oniroku
Lynch-Watson, J. The Little Red Hen
Mahlmann, L. Anansi and the Box of Stories
_____. Baba Yaga
_____. The Blue Willow
_____. The Elephant's Child
_____. The Gingerbread Boy
_____. The Legend of Urashima
_____. The Little Indian Brave
_____. Manora, the Bird Princess
_____. Perez and Martina
_____. The Rabbit Who Wanted Red Wings
_____. The Table, the Donkey and the Stick
_____. Toads and Diamonds
_____. Uncle Remus Tales
McCaslin, N. Stone Soup
_____. The Talking Cat
Nolan, P. Boshibari and the Two Thieves
_____. The Courters
_____. The Double Nine of Chih Yuan
_____. The French Cabinetmaker
_____. The Gates of Dinkelsbuehl
_____. The Golden Voice of Little Erik
_____. The Highland Fling
_____. Johnny Appleseed
_____. Licha's Birthday Serenade
_____. The Magic of Salamanca
_____. Our Sister, Sitya
_____. Robin Hood and the Match at Nottingham
_____. The Skill of Pericles
_____. The Son of William Tell
_____. Stanislaw and the Wolf
Stokes, J. Wiley and the Hairy Man
Wheetley, K. The Buffalo and the Bell
Winther, B. African Trio
_____. Ah Wing Fu and the Golden Dragon
_____. Anansi, the African Spider
_____. Fire Demon and South Wind
_____. The Great Samurai Sword
_____. Ijapa, the Tortoise
_____. Japanese Trio
_____. Listen to the Hodja
_____. Little Mouse-Deer
_____. The Maharajah Is Bored

Hark, M. Merry Christmas, Crawfords!
Lynch-Watson, J. The Lion and the Mouse
Mahlmann, L. Aesop's Fables
Spencer, S. Tom Sawyer
FROGS AND TOADS
Gilfond, H. The Celebrated Jumping Frog of Calaveras County
Mahlmann, L. Toads and Diamonds
Nicol, E. Beware the Quickly Who
From Freedom to Independence. Rembrandt, E.

- G -

Gabriel, Michelle. Chanukah Story. In Gabriel, M. Jewish Plays
    for Jewish Days. 9 char
_____. The Holiday Machine. In Gabriel, M. Jewish Plays for
    Jewish days. 14 char
_____. Little Tree Learns a Lesson. In Gabriel, M. Jewish
    Plays for Jewish Days. 12 char
_____. The Passover Predicament. In Gabriel, M. Jewish Plays
    for Jewish Days. 10 char
_____. The Purim Wax Museum. In Gabriel, M. Jewish Plays
    for Jewish Days. 7 char
_____. Sabbath Recipe. In Gabriel, M. Jewish Plays for Jewish
    Days. 8 char
_____. Shavuot. In Gabriel, M. Jewish Plays for Jewish Days.
    7 char
_____. The Spirit of Sukkot. In Gabriel, M. Jewish Plays for
    Jewish Days. 6 char
_____. The Tale of Lag B'Omer. In Gabriel, M. Jewish Plays
    for Jewish Days. 6 char
_____. This Is Your Life, Israel. In Gabriel, M. Jewish Plays
    for Jewish Days. 9 char
_____. Tisha B'av. In Gabriel, M. Jewish Plays for Jewish
    Days. 4 char
Gaines, Frederick. A Christmas Carol. In Donahue, J. and L.
    Jenkins. Five Plays from the Children's Theatre Company of
    Minneapolis. 31+ char
GAMBLING
Bradley, V. A Roll of Nickels
GAMES
Owen, D. Follow the Leader
The Garden at the Zoo. Farrar, J.
GARDENERS
Carlson, B. Rain or Shine
GARDENING
Carlson, B. Think Twice
GARDENS
Bradley, V. If the Rabbit Pickets, You're Doing Something
    Wrong
_____. Mrs. Clopsaddle Presents Spring

Mahlmann, L. Rapunzel's Tower
_____. Tale of Peter Rabbit
Garver, Juliet. Space Suit with Roses. In Kamerman, S. Space
and Science Fiction Plays for Young People. 13 char
The Gates at Dinkelsbuehl. Nolan, P.
George, the Timid Ghost. McCaslin, N.
George Washington, Farmer. Fisher, A.
GERMANY
    Carlson, B. Clever--Eh?
    Hark, M. Merry Christmas Customs
    Mahlmann, L. The Pied Piper of Hamelin
    _____. The Table, the Donkey and the Stick
    Nolan, P. The Gates of Dinkelsbuehl
Gerrold, David. The Trouble with Tribbles. In Kamerman, S.
Space and Science Fiction Plays for Young People. 18+ char
GETTYSBURG
    DuBois, G. Bonds of Affection
The Ghost of Plymouth Castle. Alexander, S.
GHOSTS
    Alexander, S. The Ghost of Plymouth Castle
    _____. Something Scary
    Beck, W. False Pretenses
    Bradley, V. The Haunted House
    _____. Here Lies McClean
    _____. The Last Bus from Lockerbee
    _____. Ludlillian and the Dark Road
    _____. The Story of John Worthington Snee
    _____. Tillie's Terror
    Fisher, A. Mr. Scrooge Finds Christmas
    Gaines, F. The Legend of Sleepy Hollow
    Gilfond, H. The Open Window
    Harris, A. Punch and Judy
    Murray, J. Old Ghosts at Home
    Olfson, L. A Christmas Carol
    Thane, A. A Christmas Carol
    Wright, R. Five Ghosts
GIANTS
    Alexander, S. Good Day, Giant!
    Nolan, P. Our Sister, Sitya
    Olfson, L. The Braggart's Clever Wife
    Rafferty, R. Jack and the Beanstalk
Gilfond, Henry. David Swan. In Gilfond, H. Walker Plays for
Reading. 18 char
The Gingerbread Boy. Mahlmann, L.
GIRL SCOUTS
    Bradley, V. Help!
GLASSES
    Marks, B. Memory Course
Glorygum. Deary, T.
GOATS
    Mahlmann, L. Three Billy Goats Gruff

GODS AND GODDESSES
>   Donahue, J.   The Cookie Jar
>   Mahlmann, L.   Anansi and the Box of Stories
>   Warren, L.   The Palmwine Drinkard
>   _____.   Woyenji
>   Winther, B.   Bata's Lessons
God's Wide Spaces.   Rembrandt, E.
GOLD
>   Fisher, A.   Sing, America, Sing
>   Mahlmann, L.   King Midas and the Golden Touch
>   _____.   King of the Golden River
>   _____.   Rumpelstiltskin
>   McCaslin, N.   The Pot of Gold
>   _____.   The Talking Cat
Golden, Joseph.   Johnny Moonbeam and the Silver Arrow.   In Jennings, C. and Harris, A.   Plays Children Love (A Treasury of Contemporary and Classic Plays for Children).   6 char
The Golden Voice of Little Erik.   Nolan, P.
Good Day, Giant!   Alexander, S.
GOVERNMENT
>   Martin, J.   The Building and the Statue
GRADUATION
>   Bradley, V.   Nothing Will Rattle a Regnant Soul
GRAND CANYON
>   Martin, J.   Big Burger
GRANDPARENTS
>   Bennett, R.   Granny Goodman's Christmas
>   McSweeny, M.   The Christmas Party
Granny Goodman's Christmas.   Bennett, R.
Great Caesar.   Beck, W.
The Great Samurai Sword.   Winther, B.
The Greater Miracle.   Bradley, V.
The Greatest Christmas Gift.   Murray, J.
GREECE
>   Mahlmann, L.   Aesop's Fables
>   Nolan, P.   The Skill of Pericles
GREED
>   Deverell, R.   The Copetown City Kite Crisis
>   Guay, G.   The Bling Said Hello
>   Mahlmann, L.   Beauty and the Beast
>   _____.   King Midas and the Golden Touch
>   _____.   King of the Golden River
>   _____.   The Pied Piper of Hamelin
>   _____.   Snow White and Rose Red
>   McCaslin, N.   The Fisherman and His Wife
>   Swortzell, L.   The Fisherman and His Wife
>   Winther, B.   White Elephant
The Green Stone.   Owen, D.
GREENE, NATHANAEL
>   Hackett, W.   Incident at Valley Forge
Grimm, Brothers.   The Shoemaker and the Elves.   In Kamerman, S.
>   On Stage for Christmas.   8 char

Grinins, Tekla. To Test the Truth. In Kamerman, S. Patriotic
    and Historical Plays for Young People. 12+ char
A Groundhog by Any Other Name. Bradley, V.
GROUNDHOG'S DAY
    Bradley, V. A Groundhog by Any Other Name...
Guay, Georgette. The Bling Said Hello. In Anonymous. Kids'
    Plays. 9 char
A Guide for George Washington. Barbee, L.
Gwendolyn Gloria Gertrude McFee. Bradley, V.

- H -

Hackett, Walter. Incident at Valley Forge. In Kamerman, S.
    Patriotic and Historical Plays for Young People. 8 char
Hail the Lucky Year. Henderson, N.
HAIR
    Mahlmann, L. Rapunzel's Tower
Half of the Reward. Carlson, B.
HALLOWEEN
    Alexander, S. Something Scary
    Bradley, V. Ludlillian and the Dark Road
    Gaines, F. The Legend of Sleepy Hollow
    Miller, H. The Broomstick Beauty
    Murray, J. Old Ghosts at Home
    Watkins, M. Nobody Believes in Witches
HANDICAPPED
    Duvall, L. The Chosen One
    Olfson, L. A Christmas Carol
    Thane, A. A Christmas Carol
    Walker, S. The Birthday of the Infanta
Hands Off! Don't Touch! Martin, J.
Hark, Mildred and Noel McQueen. Author of Liberty. In Kamer-
    man, S. Patriotic and Historical Plays for Young People. 8
    char
_____ and _____. Christmas Recaptured. In Kamerman, S.
    On Stage for Christmas. 8 char
_____ and _____. Christmas Shopping Early. In Kamerman, S.
    Holiday Plays Around the Year. 6+ char
_____ and _____. Merry Christmas, Crawfords! In Kamerman,
    S. Christmas Play Favorites for Young People. 15+ char
_____ and _____. Merry Christmas, Crawfords! In Kamerman,
    S. A Treasury of Christmas Plays. 17 char
_____ and _____. Merry Christmas Customs. In Kamerman, S.
    A Treasury of Christmas Plays. 10 char
_____ and _____. Reindeer on the Roof. In Kamerman, S.
    On Stage for Christmas. 10 char
_____ and _____. What, No Santa Claus? In Kamerman, S.
    On Stage for Christmas. 2+ char
Harriet Tubman, Conductor of the Freedom Train. Ross, L.
Harris, Aurand. Androcles and the Lion. In Harris, A. Six Plays
    for Children. 6 char

_____. Androcles and the Lion. In Jennings, C. and Harris, A. Plays Children Love (A Treasury of Contemporary and Classic Plays for Children). 6 char

_____. Ming Lee and the Magic Tree. In Jennings, C. and A. Harris. Plays Children Love. 17+ char

_____. Peck's Bad Boy. In Harris, A. Six Plays for Children. 7 char

_____. Punch and Judy. In Harris, A. Six Plays for Children. 13 char

_____. Rags to Riches. In Harris, A. Six Plays for Children. 9+ char

_____. Steal Away Home. In Harris, A. Six Plays for Children. 23+ char

_____. A Toby Show. In Jennings, C. and Harris, A. Plays Children Love. 7 char

_____. Yankee Doodle. In Harris, A. Six Plays for Children. 12 char

_____. Yankee Doodle Dandies (Johnny Appleseed, Harriet Tubman, Casey at the Bat). In Jennings, C. and A. Harris. Plays Children Love. (Johnny Appleseed--7+ char; Harriet Tubman--1+ char; Casey at the Bat--10 char)

HATS

Abisch, R. What Kind of Hat?

The Haunted House. Bradley, V.

He Won't Be Home for Christmas. Moessinger, W.

Head, Faye E. The Second Shepherd's Play. In Kamerman, S. On Stage for Christmas. 7 char

The Heart of a Monkey. Carlson, B.

The Heiress, or the Croak of Doom. Rockwell, T.

Help! Bradley, V.

Henderson, Nancy. Come to the Fair. In Henderson, N. Celebrate America: A Baker's Dozen of Plays. 24+ char

_____. Hail the Lucky Year. In Henderson, N. Celebrate America: A Baker's Dozen of Plays. 9+ char

_____. Honor the Brave. In Henderson, N. Celebrate America: A Baker's Dozen of Plays. 5 char

_____. Legend for Our Time. In Henderson, N. Celebrate America: A Baker's Dozen of Plays. 12 char

_____. Little Turtle. In Henderson, N. Celebrate America: A Baker's Dozen of Plays. 9+ char

_____. "John Muir, Earth-Planet, Universe." In Henderson, N. Celebrate America: A Baker's Dozen of Plays. 10 char

_____. Keeping Christmas Merry. In Henderson, N. Celebrate America: A Baker's Dozen of Plays. 6 char

_____. The Land We Love. In Henderson, N. Celebrate America: A Baker's Dozen of Plays. 14 char

_____. M.D. in Petticoats. In Henderson, N. Celebrate America: A Baker's Dozen of Plays. 24+ char

_____. Moonlife 2069. In Henderson, N. Celebrate America: A Baker's Dozen of Plays. 13 char

_____. Popcorn Whoppers. In Henderson, N. Celebrate America: A Baker's Dozen of Plays. 12 char

HOLOCAUST
      Rembrandt, E. So Young to Die
Home Movies. Murray, J.
Home Sweet Home Computer. Murray, J.
Home to Stay. Rembrandt, E.
HONESTY
      Carlson, B. Half of the Reward
Honor the Brave. Henderson, N.
Hooray for the Cup. Owen, D.
HOPE
      Bennett, R. Piccola
      Nolan, P. And Christmas Is Its Name
Hoppenstedt, Elbert. Santa Goes Mod. In Kamerman, S. On Stage
    for Christmas. 12+ char
_____ and Helen Waite. The Master of the Strait. In Kamerman,
    S. A Treasury of Christmas Plays. 7 char
Horse Sense. Dias, E.
HORSES
      Carlson, B. So Proud
      Dias, E. Horse Sense
      Marks, B. The Concert
      McCaslin, N. Little Indian Two Feet's Horse
HOSPITALS
      Bradley, A. Paddington Goes to the Hospital
      Murray, J. Visiting Hours
HOUSES
      Korty, C. Building the House
      Mahlmann, L. The Three Little Pigs
      McCaslin, N. The Blacksmith and the Carpenter
How Could You Tell. Donahue, J.
How Did We Manage Before the Postman Came? Bradley, V.
How to Eat Fried Worms. Rockwell, T.
Howard, Helen L. Candles for Christmas. In Kamerman, S. A
    Treasury of Christmas Plays. 6 char
Howells, William Dean. Christmas Every Day. In Kamerman, S.
    Christmas Play Favorites for Young People. 9 char
_____. Christmas Every Day. In Kamerman, S. A Treasury of
    Christmas Plays. 22 char
The Humblest Place. DuBois, G.
HUMOR
      Bradley, A. The Arrival of Paddington
      _____. Paddington Goes to the Hospital
      _____. Paddington Goes to the Launderette
      _____. Paddington Has a Birthday
      _____. Paddington Paints a Picture
      _____. Paddington Turns Detective
      Bradley, V. The Bracelet Engagement
      _____. The Carousel and a Cold Fried Egg
      _____. Herlock Sholmes
      _____. Mrs. Clapsaddle Presents Spring
      _____. The Night That Time Sat Still

- I -

An Imaginary Trial of George Washington. Wolman, D.
Imagination. Beck, W.
IMAGINATION
  Bradley, V. The Night That Time Sat Still
  Gilfond, H. Shipwreck
  Harris, A. Peck's Bad Boy
IMMIGRATION
  Henderson, N. The Land We Love
IMMIGRANTS
  Olfson, L. A Birthday Anthem for America
IMPROVISATION
  Chernak, S. The Elves and the Shoemaker
  Maloney, L. I Didn't Know That!
In One Basket. Pugh, S.
In Search of Christmas. Owen, D.
In the Kitchen of the King. Lawler, L.
Incident at Valley Forge. Hackett, W.
INDIA
  Winther, B. The Maharajah Is Bored
  _____. Pacca, the Little Bowman
  _____. Prince Rama
Indian Country. Owen, D.
INDIANS
  Bradley, V. Arizona Pilgrims
  Fisher, A. Sing the Songs of Christmas
  Golden, J. Johnny Moonbeam and the Silver Arrow
  Henderson, N. Little Turtle
  Mahlmann, L. The Little Indian Brave
  McCaslin, N. Little Indian Two Feet's Horse
  Owen, D. Indian Country
  Ross, L. Pocahontas and Captain John Smith
INDONESIA
  Nolan, P. Our Sister, Sitya
  Wheetley, K. The Buffalo and the Bell
  Winther, B. Little Mouse-Deer
INSANITY
  Rockwell, T. The Heiress, or The Croak of Doom
INSTRUMENTS
  Alexander, S. One, Two, Three!
An International Affair. Murray, J.
The Introduction. Murray, J.
INVENTIONS
  Boiko, C. Escape to the Blue Planet
IRELAND
  Bradley, V. Hibernian Picnic
  Duvall, L. Little Chip's Christmas Tree
  McCaslin, N. Stone Soup
  Murray, J. The Greatest Christmas Gift
Irving, Washington. The Legend of Sleepy Hollow. In Donahue,
  J. and L. Jenkins. Five Plays from the Children's Theatre
  Company of Minneapolis. 13+ char

Is There Life on Other Planets? Lane, M.
ISRAEL
     Gabriel, M. This Is Your Life, Israel
     Rembrandt, E. Home to Stay
ITALY
     Hark, M. Merry Christmas Customs
     Nolan, P. The Courters
It's a Mystery to Me. Murray, J.
It's Magic. Murray, J.

- J -

Jack and the Beanstalk. Rafferty, R.
Jagendorf, Moritz. Bumbo and Scrumbo, and Blinko. In Jagendorf,
    M. A., ed. One-Act Plays for Young Folks. 4 char
    _____. Once in a Hundred Years. In Jagendorf, M. One-Act
    Plays for Young Folks. 7 char
JAMESTOWN
     Ross, L. Pocahontas and Captain John Smith
Janney, Sam. The East Wind's Revenge. In Jagendorf, M. One-
    Act Plays for Young Folks. 11 char
JAPAN
     Carlson, B. Think Twice
     Jagendorf, M. Once in a Hundred Years
     Kraus, J. The Tale of Oniroku
     Mahlmann, L. The Legend of Urashima
     McCaslin, N. The Lantern and the Fan
     Nolan, P. Boshibari and the Two Thieves
     Shaw, R. Sleeping Beauty
     Winther, B. The Great Samurai Sword
     _____. Japanese Trio
Japanese Trio. Winther, B.
JAVA
     Nolan, P. Our Sister, Sitya
JEFFERSON, THOMAS
     Fisher, A. Ask Mr. Jefferson
     Hark, M. Author of Liberty
     Slingluff, M. Naughty Susan
Jensen, Stanley C. North Pole Confidential. In Kamerman, S.
    A Treasury of Christmas Plays. 9 char
JESTERS
     Bradley, V. Nester the Jester
JESUS CHRIST
     McGowan, J. The Coming of the Prince
JESUS CHRIST--NATIVITY
     Cavanah, F. The Transfiguration of the Gifts
     DuBois, G. The Humblest Place
     _____. A Room for a King
     _____. Star Over Bethlehem

- K -

KABUKI (JAPANESE DRAMA)
>   Shaw, R.   Sleeping Beauty
>   Winther, B.   The Great Samurai Sword
> Kamerman, Sylvia.   Nine Cheers for Christmas.   In Kamerman, S.
>   A Treasury of Christmas Plays.   19 char
> Kane, Eleanora.   Paul Revere of Boston.   In Kamerman, S.   Patriotic
>   and Historical Plays for Young Poeple.   17 char
> Keeping Christmas.   Peacock, M.
> Keeping Christmas Merry.   Henderson, N.
KEY, FRANCIS SCOTT
>   Miller, H.   Old Glory Grows Up
> Kiddie Matinee.   Murray, J.
> Kidnapped in London.   Mason, T.
KIDNAPPING
>   Alexander, S.   The Case of the Kidnapped Nephew
>   Campbell, P.   Chinook
>   Mason, T.   Kidnapped in London
>   McSweeny, M.   Listen to the Peace and Goodwill
>   Sergel, K.   Winnie-the-Pooh
KINDNESS
>   Bradley, A.   The Arrival of Paddington
>   Bradley, V.   The Big Red Heart
>   Carlson, B.   The Heart of a Monkey
>   _____.   The Tiger, the Brahman, and the Jackal
>   Dias, E.   Christmas Spirit
>   Gaines, F.   A Christmas Carol
>   Hackett, W.   A Merry Christmas
>   Hark, M.   Merry Christmas, Crawfords!
>   Harris, A.   Androcles and the Lion
>   _____.   Steal Away Home
>   Lynch-Watson, J.   The Lion and the Mouse
>   Mahlmann, L.   Aesop's Fables
>   _____.   Beauty and the Beast
>   _____.   Cinderella
>   _____.   King of the Golden River
>   _____.   The Legend of Urashima
>   _____.   Snow White and Rose Red
>   Martens, A.   Star of Bethlehem
>   Morley, O.   Little Women
>   Nolan, P.   Johnny Appleseed
>   Olfson, L.   Nine Times Christmas
>   Very, A.   The Shoemaker and the Elves
>   Wilson, E.   The Least of These
>   Winther, B.   Pacca, the Little Bowman
KING, CORETTA SCOTT
>   Henderson, N.   Soul Force
KING, MARTIN LUTHER (JUNIOR)
>   Henderson, N.   Soul Force
> King Midas and the Golden Touch.   Mahlmann, L.

The King of Tarantulus. Deary, T.
King of the Golden River. Mahlmann, L.
KINGS AND QUEENS
    Atherton, M. Old King Cole's Christmas
    Barr, J. A White Christmas
    Bradley, V. Flat, Flat, Flat
    _____. Nester the Jester
    Carlson, B. Anyone Could, but---
    Deary, T. The King of Tarantulus
    Lynch-Watson, J. The Emperor's New Clothes
    Mahlmann, L. King Midas and the Golden Touch
    _____. King of the Golden River
    _____. The Nutcracker Prince
    _____. Rumpelstiltskin
    Murray, J. The Greatest Christmas Gift
    Nolan, P. Our Sister, Sitya
    Owen, D. The Green Stone
    _____. The Magic Peacock
    Rockwell, T. Myron Mere
    Warren, L. Woyenji
    White, J. Snow White and the Seven Dwarfs
    Winther, B. Fire Demon and South Wind
    _____. The Flying Horse Machine
    _____. Follow the River Lai
    _____. Pacca, the Little Bowman
    Wright, D. The Twelve Days of Christmas
Kipling, Rudyard. The Elephant's Child. In Mahlmann, L. and D.
    Jones. Puppet Plays from Favorite Stories. 9 char
KNIGHTS
    Bradley, V. Nester the Jester
    Runnette, H. Touchstone
KOREA
    Kraus, J. The Dragon Hammer
    Winther, B. Fire Demon and South Wind
Korty, Carol. Ananse's Trick Does Double Work. In Korty, C.
    Plays from African Folktales. 5 char
_____. Bag of Gold. In Korty, C. Silly Soup: Ten Zany Plays
    with Songs and Ideas for Making Them Your Own. 3 char
_____. Building the House. In Korty, C. Silly Soup: Ten Zany
    Plays with Songs and Ideas for Making Them Your Own. 5 char
_____. Clever Clyde. In Korty, C. Silly Soup: Ten Zany
    Plays with Songs and Ideas for Making Them Your Own. 5 char
_____. The Flagpole. In Korty, C. Silly Soup: Ten Zany
    Plays with Songs and Ideas for Making Them Your Own. 3 char
_____. Jogging. In Korty, C. Silly Soup: Ten Zany Plays
    with Songs and Ideas for Making Them Your Own. 2 char
_____. The Man Who Loved to Laugh. In Korty, C. Plays from
    African Folktales. 11+ char
_____. Mr. Hare Takes Mr. Leopard for a Ride. In Korty, C.
    Plays from African Folktales. 3 char
_____. Moon Shot. In Korty, C. Silly Soup: Ten Zany Plays
    with Songs and Ideas for Making Them Your Own. 5 char

_____. Opera Singer. In Korty, C. Silly Soup: Ten Zany
Plays with Songs and Ideas for Making Them Your Own. 3 char
_____. The Pumpkin. In Korty, C. Silly Soup: Ten Zany
Plays with Songs and Ideas for Making Them Your Own. 4 char
_____. The Road to Market. In Korty, C. Silly Soup: Ten
Zany Plays with Songs and Ideas for Making Them Your Own.
3 char
_____. Stretch the Bench. In Korty, C. Silly Soup: Ten Zany
Plays with Songs and Ideas for Making Them Your Own. 4 char
_____. The Turtle Who Wanted to Fly. In Korty, C. Plays from
African Folktales. 3 char
Kraus, Joanna. The Dragon Hammer. In Kraus, J. The Dragon
Hammer and the Tale of Oniroku. 12 char
_____. The Tale of Oniroku. In Kraus, J. The Dragon Hammer
and the Tale of Oniroku. 12 char

- L -

The Lady or the Tiger. Gilford, H.
LAFAYETTE, MARQUIS DE
        Fisher, A. Washington Marches On
The Land We Love. Henderson, N.
Lane, Marion. Is There Life on Other Planets? In Kamerman, S.
        Space and Science Fiction Plays for Young People. 6 char
The Lantern. Brown, A.
The Lantern and the Fan. McCaslin, N.
The Last Bus from Lockerbee. Bradley, V.
The Last Leaf. Gilford, H.
The Last Leaf. Henry, O.
LAUGHTER
        Alexander, S. Tricky Gifts
        Bradley, V. Nester the Jester
        Korty, C. The Man Who Loved to Laugh
The Law of the Jungle. Carlson, B.
Lawler, Lillian. In the Kitchen of the King. In Jagendorf, M.
        One-Act Plays for Young Folks. 13+ char
A Leak in the Dike. Nolan, P.
The Least of These. Wilson, E. and Field, A.
The Left-Over Reindeer. Miller, H.
Legend for Our Time. Henderson, N.
The Legend of Sleepy Hollow. Irving, W.
The Legend of the Christmas Rose. Leuser, E.
The Legend of Urashima. Mahlmann, L.
LEGENDS
        Campbell, P. Chinook
        Gaines, F. The Legend of Sleepy Hollow
        Henderson, N. Hail the Lucky Year
        Mahlmann, L. The Pied Piper of Hamelin
        Mason, T. Robin Hood: A Story of the Forest
        Nolan, P. Johnny Appleseed

_____. A Leak in the Dike
_____. The Son of William Tell
Winther, B. Abu Nuwas
_____. Follow the River Lai
_____. John Henry
The Leprechaun Shoemaker. Watts, F.
LEPRECHAUNS
     Murray, J. The Greatest Christmas Gift
     Watts, F. The Leprechaun Shoemaker
Let George Do It. Pendleton, E.
Leuser, Eleanor D. The Christmas Sampler. In Kamerman, S. A
    Treasury of Christmas Plays. 10+ char
_____. The Legend of the Christmas Rose. In Kamerman, S.
    A Treasury of Christmas Plays. 10+ char
LIBERTY
     Fisher, A. Ask Mr. Jefferson
     Slingluff, M. Naughty Susan
LIBERTY BELL
     Slingluff, M. Naughty Susan
LIBRARIES
     Chaloner, G. The Bookworm
     Fisher, A. Ask Mr. Jefferson
Licha's Birthday Serenade. Nolan, P.
LINCOLN, ABRAHAM
     Bradley, V. Abe Lincoln: Star Center
     DuBois, G. Bonds of Affection
     Grinins, T. To Test the Truth
     Smith, B. The Boy, Abe
     Watson, W. Abe and the Runaways
LINCOLN'S BIRTHDAY
     DuBois, G. Bonds of Affection
     Smith, B. The Boy, Abe
The Lion and the Mouse. Lynch-Watson, J.
Lion, Sick and Dying. Carlson, B.
Listen to the Hodja. Winther, B.
Listen to the Peace and Goodwill. McSweeny, M.
Little Chip's Christmas Tree. Duvall, L.
Little Girls Wiser Than Men. Gilford, H.
The Little Indian Brave. Mahlmann, L.
Little Indian Two Feet's Horse. McCaslin, N.
The Little Man Who Wasn't There. Dias, E.
Little Mouse-Deer. Winther, B.
The Little Red Hen. Lynch-Watson, J.
The Little Shadows. Brown, A. F.
Little Tree Learns a Lesson. Gabriel, M.
Little Turtle. Henderson, N.
Little Women. Alcott, L. M.
Little Women. Alcott, L. (Play title: Keeping Christmas Merry,
    written by Henderson, N.)
The Looking Glass Murder. Murray, J.
LOVE
     Callanan, C. Cupid and Company

Dias, E. The Little Man Who Wasn't There
Gilfond, H. The Romance of a Busy Broker
Harris, A. Androcles and the Lion
Mahlmann, L. Aesop's Fables
_____ . Beauty and the Beast
_____ . The Blue Willow
_____ . Cinderella
_____ . Sleeping Beauty
_____ . Snow White and Rose Red
McGowan, J. Miss Lonelyheart
Nolan, P. The Courters
Pendleton, E. 'Twas the Night Before Christmas
Ross, L. Pocahontas and Captain John Smith
Shaw, R. Sleeping Beauty
White, J. Snow White and the Seven Dwarfs

LOYALTY
Murray, J. The Looking Glass Murder
Ross, L. Pocahontas and Captain John Smith

LUCK
Winther, B. White Elephant
Ludlillian and the Dark Road. Bradley, V.

LUTHER, MARTIN
Hark, M. Merry Christmas Customs
Lynch-Watson, Janet. The Lion and the Mouse. In Lynch-Watson,
J. The Shadow Puppet Book. 3 char
_____ . The Little Red Hen. In Lynch-Watson, J. The Shadow
Puppet Book. 6 char

- M -

Ma and the Kids. Martin, J.
MACCABEE, JUDAH
Gabriel, M. Chanukah Story
MAGIC
Alexander, S. Whatever Happened to Uncle Albert?
Bradley, A. Paddington Has a Birthday
DeRegniers, B. The Magic Spell
_____ . The Mysterious Stranger
Kraus, J. The Dragon Hammer
Mahlmann, L. Aladdin, or The Wonderful Lamp
_____ . Beauty and the Beast
_____ . Cinderella
_____ . King Midas and the Golden Touch
_____ . Snow White and Rose Red
_____ . The Table, the Donkey and the Stick
_____ . Toads and Diamonds
Marks, B. The Beauty Potion
Murray, J. It's Magic
Olfson, L. The Old Woman of the West
Owen, D. The Magic Peacock

Ringwood, G. The Magic Carpets of Antonio Angelini
Stokes, J. Wiley and the Hairy Man
Swortzell, L. The Fisherman and His Wife
Thane, A. The Christmas Nutcracker
Warren, L. Woyenji
Watkins, M. Nobody Believes in Witches
Winther, B. Fire Demon and South Wind
_____. The Flying Horse Machine
_____. Ijapa, the Tortoise
_____. Two Dilemma Tales
The Magic Carpets of Antonio Angelini. Ringwood, G.
The Magic of Salamanca. Nolan, P.
The Magic Peacock. Owen, D.
The Magic Spell. DeRegniers, B.
MAGICIANS
Abisch, R. What Kind of Hat?
Olfson, L. The Braggart's Clever Wife
The Maharajah Is Bored. Winther, B.
Mahlmann, Lewis. Aesop's Fables. In Mahlmann, L. and D. Jones.
Puppet Plays from Favorite Stories. 11 char
_____. Aladdin, or the Wonderful Lamp. In Mahlmann, L. and
Jones, D. Puppet Plays from Favorite Stories. 7 char
_____. Ali Baba and the Forty Thieves. In Mahlmann, L. and
Jones, D. Folk Tale Plays for Puppets. 7 char
_____. Anansi and the Box of Stories. In Mahlmann, L. and
Jones, D. Folk Tale Plays for Puppets. 5 char
_____. Baba Yaga. In Mahlmann, L. and Jones, D. Folk Tale
Plays for Puppets. 7 char
_____. Beauty and the Beast. In Mahlmann, L. and D. Jones.
Puppet Plays from Favorite Stories. 11+ char
_____. The Blue Willow. In Mahlmann, L. and D. Jones. Folk
Tale Plays for Puppets. 10 char
_____. Cinderella. In Mahlmann, L. and Jones, D. Puppet
Plays from Favorite Stories. 8 char
_____. The Gingerbread Boy. In Mahlmann, L. and D. Jones.
Folk Tale Plays for Puppets. 10 char
_____. King Midas and the Golden Touch. In Mahlmann, L. and
Jones, D. Puppet Plays from Favorite Stories. 7 char
_____. The Legend of Urashima. In Mahlmann, L. and Jones, D.
Folk Tale Plays for Puppets. 9 char
_____. The Little Indian Brave. In Mahlmann, L. and D. Jones.
Folk Tale Plays for Puppets. 10 char
_____. Manora, the Bird Princess. In Mahlmann, L. and D.
Jones. Folk Tale Plays for Puppets. 11 char
_____. The Nutcracker Princess. In Mahlmann, L. and D.
Jones. Puppet Plays from Favorite Stories. 13+ char
_____. Perez and Martina. In Mahlmann, L. and D. Jones.
Puppet Plays from Favorite Stories. 12+ char
_____. The Pied Piper of Hamelin. In Mahlmann, L. and D.
Jones. Puppet Plays from Favorite Stories. 13+ char
_____. The Rabbit Who Wanted Red Wings. In Mahlmann, L. and
D. Jones. Folk Tale Plays for Puppets. 8 char

_____. Rapunzel's Tower. In Mahlmann, L. and D. Jones. Puppet Plays from Favorite Stories. 8 char
_____. Rumpelstiltskin. In Mahlmann, L. and D. Jones. Puppet Plays from Favorite Stories. 6 char
_____. Sleeping Beauty. In Mahlmann, L. and D. Jones. Puppet Plays from Favorite Stories. 12 char
_____. Snow White and Rose Red. In Mahlmann, L. and D. Jones. Puppet Plays from Favorite Stories. 8 char
_____. The Table, the Donkey and the Stick. In Mahlmann, L. and D. Jones. Folk Tale Plays for Puppets. 9 char
_____. Three Billy Goats Gruff. In Mahlmann, L. and D. Jones. Puppet Plays from Favorite Stories. 7 char
_____. The Three Little Pigs. In Mahlmann, L. and D. Jones. Puppet Plays from Favorite Stories. 5 char
_____. Toads and Diamonds. In Mahlmann, L. and D. Jones. Folk Tale Plays for Puppets. 7 char
_____. Uncle Remus Tales. In Mahlmann, L. and D. Jones. Folk Tale Plays for Puppets. 7 char
Majeski, Bill. Whatever Happened to Good Old Ebenezer Scrooge? In Kamerman, S. On Stage for Christmas. 14 char
Maloney, L., J. Saldana, J. Selber, and R. Winfree. I Didn't Know That! In Jennings, C. and Aurand Harris. Plays Children Love. 5 char
Man in the Red Suit. Moessenger, B.
The Man Who Loved to Laugh. Korty, C.
Manora, the Bird Princess. Mahlmann, L.
Marks, Burton and Rita Marks. The Beauty Potion. In Marks, B. & R. Puppet Plays and Puppet-Making. 3 char
_____ and _____. The Concert. In Marks, B. & R. Puppet Plays and Puppet-Making. 3 char
_____ and _____. The Cooking Lesson. In, Marks, B. & R. Puppet Plays and Puppet-Making. 2 char
_____ and _____. Memory Course. In Marks, B. & R. Puppet Plays and Puppet-Making. 2 char
_____ and _____. The Rope. In Marks, B. & R. Puppet Plays and Puppet-Making. 2 char
Marks, Rita and Burton Marks. The Beauty Potion. In Marks, B. & R. Puppet Plays and Puppet-Making. 3 char
_____ and _____. The Concert. In Marks, B. & R. Puppet Plays and Puppet-Making. 3 char
_____ and _____. The Cooking Lesson. In Marks, B. & R. Puppet Plays and Puppet-Making. 2 char
_____ and _____. Memory Course. In Marks, B. & R. Puppet Plays and Puppet-Making. 2 char
_____ and _____. The Rope. In Marks, B. & R. Puppet Plays and Puppet-Making. 2 char
Marlens, Anne. Visions of Sugar Plums. In Kamerman, S. Christmas Play Favorites for Young People. 7 char
Marra, Dorothy Brandt. "Woof" for the Red, White, and Blue. In Kamerman, S. Patriotic and Historical Plays for Young People. 5 char

MARRIAGE
>Pugh, S. In One Basket
>Warren, L. The Palmwine Drinkard
>Winther, B. The Great Samurai Sword

MARS
>Watts, F. High Fashion from Mars

Marshall, Sheila L. The Year Santa Forgot Christmas. In Kamerman, S. On Stage for Christmas. 11+ char

Martens, Anne Coulter. Santa Claus Is Twins. In Kamerman, S. On Stage for Christmas. 9+ char

_____. Star of Bethlehem. In Kamerman, S. Christmas Play Favorites for Young People. 26+ char

Martha Washington's Spy. Dias, E.

Martin, Judith. Big Burger. In Martin, J. Everybody, Everybody. 6 char

_____. Blown Off the Billboard. In Martin, J. Everybody, Everybody. 6 char

_____. The Building and the Statue. In Martin, J. Everybody, Everybody. 5 char

_____. The Chicken and the Egg. In Martin, J. Everybody, Everybody. 4+ char

_____. Everybody, Everybody. In Martin, J. Everybody, Everybody. 4 char

_____. Hands Off! Don't Touch! In Jennings, C. and A. Harris. Plays Children Love (A Treasury of Contemporary and Classic Plays for Children). 4 char

_____. I Won't Take a Bath. In Martin, J. Everybody, Everybody. 5 char

_____. Ma and the Kids. In Jennings, C. and A. Harris. Plays Children Love (A Treasury of Contemporary and Classic Plays for Children). 4 char

_____. Ma and the Kids. In Martin, J. Everybody, Everybody. 4 char

_____. That's Good, That's Good. In Martin, J. Everybody, Everybody. 4 char

Mason, Timothy. Kidnapped in London. In Donahue, J. and L. Jenkins. Five Plays from the Children's Theatre Company of Minneapolis. 19+ char.

_____. Robin Hood: A Story of the Forest. In Donahue, J. and L. Jenkins. Five Plays from the Children's Theatre Company of Minneapolis. 26+ char

The Master of the Strait. Waite, H. and E. Hoppenstedt

MAYFLOWER
>Young, S. Ship Forever Sailing

Mayr, Grace. Paul Revere, Rider to Lexington. In Kamerman, S. Patriotic and Historical Plays for Young People. 16 char

_____. The Printer in Queen Street. In Kamerman, S. Patriotic and Historical Plays for Young People. 10 char

McCaslin, Nellie. The Blacksmith and the Carpenter. In McCaslin, N. Puppet Fun. 6 char

_____. George the Timid Ghost. In McCaslin, N. Puppet Fun. 2 char

_____. The Lantern and the Fan. In McCaslin, N. Puppet
Fun. 3 char
_____. Little Indian Two Feet's Horse. In McCaslin, N. Puppet
Fun. 2 char
_____. The Pot of Gold. In McCaslin, N. Puppet Fun. 3 char
_____. Stone Soup. In McCaslin, N. Puppet Fun. 2 char
_____. The Talking Cat. In McCaslin, N. Puppet Fun. 4 char
McGowan, Jane. Bunnies and Bonnets. In Kamerman, S. Holiday
Plays Around the Year. 15+ char
_____. Miss Lonelyheart. In Kamerman, S. Holiday Plays
Around the Year. 8 char
_____. Santa Claus for President. In Kamerman, S. Christmas
Play Favorites for Young People. 18 char
_____. The Santa Claus Twins. In Kamerman, S. Christmas
Play Favorites for Young People. 15+ char
McQueen, Noel and Mildred Hark. Author of Liberty. In Kamerman,
S. Patriotic and Historical Plays for Young People. 8 char
_____ and _____. Christmas Shopping Early. In Kamerman, S.
Holiday Plays Around the Year. 6+ char
_____ and _____. Merry Christmas, Crawfords! In Kamerman,
S. Christmas Play Favorites for Young People. 15+ char
_____ and _____. Merry Christmas, Crawfords! In Kamerman,
S. A Treasury of Christmas Plays. 15+ char
_____ and _____. Merry Christmas Customs. In Kamerman, S.
A Treasury of Christmas Plays. 10 char
_____ and _____. Reindeer on the Roof. In Kamerman, S.
On Stage for Christmas. 10 char
_____ and _____. What, No Santa Claus? In Kamerman, S.
On Stage for Christmas. 2+ char
McSweeny, Maxine. The Christmas Party. In McSweeny, M. Christ-
mas Plays for Young Players. 12 char
_____. Listen to the Peace and Goodwill. In McSweeny, M.
Christmas Plays for Young Players. 10 char
_____. Santa! Please Get Up. In McSweeny, M. Christmas
Plays for Young Players. 14 char
M.D. in Petticoats. Henderson, N.
MEDIEVAL MIRACLE PLAYS
    Head, F. The Second Shepherd's Play
MELODRAMA
    Bradley, V. Tillie's Terror
    Harris, A. Rags to Riches
    _____. A Toby Show
    Winther, B. The Villain and the Toy Shop
MEMORIAL DAY
    Henderson, N. Honor the Brave
Memory Course. Marks, B. & R.
Meow! and Arf! Alexander, S.
MERMAIDS
    Bradley, V. Shoes and Ships and a Mermaid
A Merry Christmas. Alcott, L. M.
Merry Christmas, Crawfords! Hark, M. and Noel McQueen

Merry Christmas Customs. Hark, M. and N. McQueen
MEXICO
      Mahlmann, L. Perez and Martina
      Nolan, P. Licha's Birthday Serenade
      Peterson, M. Adobe Christmas
MICE
      Carlson, B. Belling the Cat
      _____. The Country Mouse and the City Mouse
      Lynch-Watson, J. The Lion and the Mouse
      Mahlmann, L. Perez and Martina
      Pugh, S. In One Basket
      Rockwell, T. Myron Mere
MIDDLE AGES
      Mahlmann, L. The Pied Piper of Hamelin
      Mason, T. Robin Hood: A Story of the Forest
      Nolan, P. Robin Hood and the Match at Nottingham
      Rockwell, T. Myron Mere
      Wright, D. The Twelve Days of Christmas
Miller, Helen. The Broomstick Beauty. In Kamerman, S. Holiday
    Plays Around the Year. 6 char
    _____. A Christmas Promise. In Kamerman, S. On Stage for
    Christmas. 6 char
    _____. The Left-Over Reindeer. In Kamerman, S. A Treasury
    of Christmas Plays. 11+ char
    _____. Mr. Snow White's Thanksgiving. In Kamerman, S. Holi-
    day Plays Around the Year. 7 char
    _____. Monsieur Santa Claus. In Kamerman, S. A Treasury of
    Christmas Plays. 16 char
    _____. Old Glory Grows Up. In Kamerman, S. Patriotic and
    Historical Plays for Young People. 19 char
    _____. Puppy Love. In Kamerman, S. Christmas Play Favorites
    for Young People. 7 char
    _____. Red Carpet Christmas. In Kamerman, S. On Stage for
    Christmas. 12 char
    _____. Season's Greetings. In Kamerman, S. A Treasury of
    Christmas Plays. 11 char
    _____. Strictly Puritan. In Kamerman, S. Holiday Plays
    Around the Year. 11 char
Miller, Patsy and Cheryl M. Thurston. Christmas at the O.K. Cor-
    ral. In Kamerman, S. Holiday Plays Around the Year. 10+
    char
Mills, Grace E. Christmas Comes to Hamelin. In Kamerman, S.
    Christmas Play Favorites for Young People. 25+ char
Ming Lee and the Magic Tree. Harris, A.
Miss Lacey and the President. Bradley, V.
Miss Lonelyheart. McGowan, J.
Mr. Bunny's Prize. Cavannah, F.
Mr. Hare Takes Mr. Leopard for a Ride. Korty, C.
Mr. Scrooge Finds Christmas. Fisher, A.
Mr. Snow White's Thanksgiving. Miller, H.
Mrs. Claus' Christmas Present. Urban, C.

Mrs. Clopsaddle Presents Christmas. Bradley, V.
Mrs. Clopsaddle Presents Spring. Bradley, V.
Mrs. Snooty and the Waiter. Abisch, R.
Model Plane. Murray, J.
Moessenger, Bill. Man in the Red Suit. In Kamerman, S. Holiday
    Plays Around the Year. 14+ char
Moessinger, William. He Won't Be Home for Christmas. In Kamer-
    man, S. On Stage for Christmas. 15+ char
Molly Pitcher. Fisher, A.
Molly Pitcher Meets the General. Hall, M.
MONEY
        Beck, W. False Pretenses
        Bradley, V. Five Times Sue Is Julia Bates
        Deary, T. The Factory
        Fisher, A. A Dish of Green Peas
        Olfson, L. A Christmas Carol
        Thane, A. A Christmas Carol
The Monkey Without a Tail. Winther, B.
MONOLOGUES
        Murray, J. Bargain Day.
        _____. A Case for Two Detectives
        _____. Den Mother
        _____. Do or Diet
        _____. The Driving Lesson
        _____. Even a Child Can Do It
        _____. First Day at School
        _____. The Fish Story
        _____. For Art's Sake
        _____. The Highway Restaurant
        _____. Home Movies
        _____. The Introduction
        _____. It's Magic
        _____. Kiddie Matinee
        _____. Model Plane
        _____. Mother of the Bride
        _____. Moving Day
        _____. No Experience
        _____. Opening Night
        _____. Space Flight to Saturn
        _____. The Super-Duper Market
        _____. Visiting Hours
Monsieur Santa Claus. Miller, H.
MONSTERS
        Bradley, V. Beware of the Glump
        _____. Torko the Terrible
        Rockwell, T. AIIIEEEEEEEEE!
        Winther, B. Fire Demon and South Wind
MOON
        Henderson, N. Moonlife 2069
        Korty, C. Moon Shot
Moon Shot. Korty, C.

Moonlife 2069. Henderson, N.
Moore, Clement C. A Visit from St. Nicholas. In Kamerman, S.
    On Stage for Christmas. 22 char
Morley, Olive J. O Little Town of Bethlehem. In Kamerman, S.
    A Treasury of Christmas Plays. 11+ char
MOTHER GOOSE
        Shipley, J. Mother Goose Drops In
Mother Goose Drops In. Shipley, J.
Mother of the Bride. Murray, J.
MOTHERS
        Warren, L. Woyenji
MOVIES
        Murray, J. Home Movies
        _____. Kiddie Matinee
Moving Day. Murray, J.
MURDER
        Murray, J. A Case for Two Detectives
        _____. Dead of Night
        _____. The Final Curtain
        _____. I Want to Report a Murder
        _____. The Looking Glass Murder
        _____. The Sixth Juror
        Spencer, S. Tom Sawyer
Murray, John. Airport Adventure. In Murray, J. Mystery Plays
    for Young Actors. 9+ char
_____. Bargain Day. In Murray, J. Modern Monologues for
    Young People. 1 char
_____. A Case for Two Detectives. In Murray, J. Modern
    Monologues for Young People. 1 char
_____. A Case for Two Detectives. In Murray, J. Mystery
    Plays for Young Actors. 12 char
_____. Dead of Night. In Murray, J. Mystery Plays for Young
    Actors. 6 char
_____. Den Mother. In Murray, J. Modern Monologues for
    Young People. 1 char
_____. Do or Diet. In Murray, J. Modern Monologues for
    Young People. 1 char
_____. The Door. In Murray, J. Mystery Plays for Young Ac-
    tors. 3 char
_____. The Driving Lesson. In Murray, J. Modern Monologues
    for Young People. 1 char
_____. Even a Child Can Do It. In Murray, J. Modern Mono-
    logues for Young People. 1 char
_____. The Final Curtain. In Murray, J. Mystery Plays for
    Young Actors. 11+ char
_____. First Day at School. In Murray, J. Modern Monologues
    for Young People. 1 char
_____. The Fish Story. In Murray, J. Modern Monologues for
    Young People. 1 char
_____. Flight International. In Murray, J. Mystery Plays for
    Young Actors. 16+ char

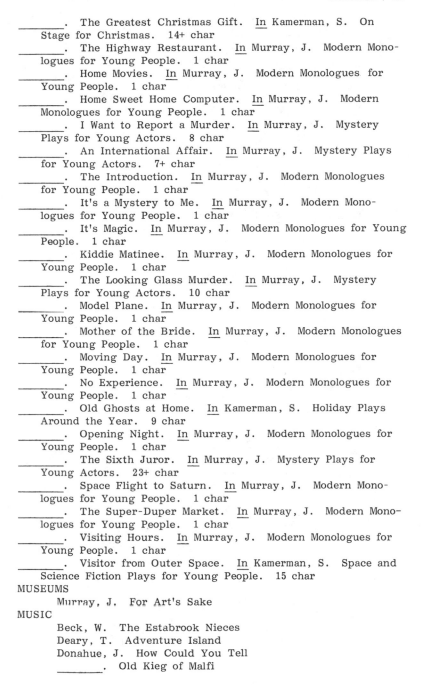

_____. The Greatest Christmas Gift. In Kamerman, S. On Stage for Christmas. 14+ char

_____. The Highway Restaurant. In Murray, J. Modern Monologues for Young People. 1 char

_____. Home Movies. In Murray, J. Modern Monologues for Young People. 1 char

_____. Home Sweet Home Computer. In Murray, J. Modern Monologues for Young People. 1 char

_____. I Want to Report a Murder. In Murray, J. Mystery Plays for Young Actors. 8 char

_____. An International Affair. In Murray, J. Mystery Plays for Young Actors. 7+ char

_____. The Introduction. In Murray, J. Modern Monologues for Young People. 1 char

_____. It's a Mystery to Me. In Murray, J. Modern Monologues for Young People. 1 char

_____. It's Magic. In Murray, J. Modern Monologues for Young People. 1 char

_____. Kiddie Matinee. In Murray, J. Modern Monologues for Young People. 1 char

_____. The Looking Glass Murder. In Murray, J. Mystery Plays for Young Actors. 10 char

_____. Model Plane. In Murray, J. Modern Monologues for Young People. 1 char

_____. Mother of the Bride. In Murray, J. Modern Monologues for Young People. 1 char

_____. Moving Day. In Murray, J. Modern Monologues for Young People. 1 char

_____. No Experience. In Murray, J. Modern Monologues for Young People. 1 char

_____. Old Ghosts at Home. In Kamerman, S. Holiday Plays Around the Year. 9 char

_____. Opening Night. In Murray, J. Modern Monologues for Young People. 1 char

_____. The Sixth Juror. In Murray, J. Mystery Plays for Young Actors. 23+ char

_____. Space Flight to Saturn. In Murray, J. Modern Monologues for Young People. 1 char

_____. The Super-Duper Market. In Murray, J. Modern Monologues for Young People. 1 char

_____. Visiting Hours. In Murray, J. Modern Monologues for Young People. 1 char

_____. Visitor from Outer Space. In Kamerman, S. Space and Science Fiction Plays for Young People. 15 char

MUSEUMS

    Murray, J. For Art's Sake

MUSIC

    Beck, W. The Estabrook Nieces

    Deary, T. Adventure Island

    Donahue, J. How Could You Tell

    _____. Old Kieg of Malfi

- N -

NATIONAL ANTHEM
    Fisher, A.   Sing, America, Sing
NATIONAL LIBRARY WEEK
    Chaloner, G.   The Bookworm
NATURE
    Brown, A.   The Wishing Moon
    Henderson, N.   "John Muir, Earth-Planet, Universe"
    Nolan, T.   The Highland Fling
Naughty Susan.   Slingluff, M.
The Necklace.   deMaupassant, G.
NEIGHBORS
    Dias, E.   Christmas Spirit
    Hark, M.   Merry Christmas, Crawfords!
Nester the Jester.   Bradley, V.
A New Angle on Christmas.   Albert, R.
NEW YEAR'S
    Bradley, V.   The Night That Time Sat Still
NEW YORK
    Dias, E.   The Christmas Starlet
Newman, Deborah.   The Christmas Question.   In Kamerman, S.
    Holiday Plays Around the Year.   2+ char
_____.   The Runaway Robots.   In Kamerman, S.   Space and Sci-
    ence Fiction Plays for Young People.   10+ char
NEWSPAPERS
    Albert, R.   A New Angle on Christmas
    Fisher, A.   When Freedom Was News
    Mayr, G.   The Printer in Queen Street
    Nolan, P.   The Trial of Peter Zenger
Next Stop, Saturn.   Fontaine, R.
Nicholson, Jessie.   Holiday for Santa.   In Kamerman, S.   A Treasury
    of Christmas Plays.   9 char
Nicol, Eric.   Beware the Quickly Who.   In Anonymous.   Kids Plays.
    12 char
NIGERIA
    Winther, B.   Ijapa, the Tortoise
The Night Time Stood Still.   Bradley, V.
Nine Cheers for Christmas.   Kamerman, S.
Nine Times Christmas.   Jokai, M.
No Experience.   Murray, J.
No Room at the Inn.   Patterson, E.
Nobody Believes in Witches.   Watkins, M.
Nolan, Paul T.   And Christmas Is Its Name.   In Kamerman, S.
    Christmas Play Favorites for Young People.   23+ char
_____.   Boshibari and the Two Thieves.   In Nolan, P.   Folk Tale
    Plays Round the World.   3 char
_____.   The Courters.   In Nolan, P.   Folk Tale Plays Round the
    World.   6 char

_____. The Double Nine of Chih Yuan. In Nolan, P. Folk Tale Plays Round the World. 5 char
_____. The French Cabinetmaker. In Nolan, P. Folktale Plays Round the World. 8 char
_____. The Gates of Dinkelsbuehl. In Nolan, P. Folktale Plays Round the World. 8+ char
_____. The Golden Voice of Little Erik. In Nolan, P. Folktale Plays Round the World. 9+ char
_____. The Highland Fling. In Nolan, P. Folk Tale Plays Round the World. 8+ char
_____. Johnny Appleseed. In Nolan, P. Folktale Plays Round the World. 9 char
_____. A Leak in the Dike. In Nolan, P. Folktale Plays Round the World. 8 char
_____. Licha's Birthday Serenade. In Nolan, P. Folk Tale Plays Round the World. 14 char
_____. The Magic of Salamanca. In Nolan, P. Folk Tale Plays Round the World. 6 char
_____. Our Sister, Sitya. In Nolan, P. Folk Tale Plays Round the World. 8 char
_____. Robin Hood and the Match at Nottingham. In Nolan, P. Folk Tale Plays Round the World. 10+ char
_____. The Skill of Pericles. In Nolan, P. Folk Tale Plays Round the World. 10+ char
_____. The Son of William Tell. In Nolan, P. Folk Tale Plays Round the World. 11 char
_____. Stanislaw and the Wolf. In Nolan, P. Folktale Plays Round the World. 9 char
_____. The Trial of Peter Zenger. In Kamerman, S. Patriotic and Historical Plays for Young People. 16+ char
_____. The Trouble with Christmas. In Kamerman, S. A Treasury of Christmas Plays. 7 char; Kamerman, S. On Stage for Christmas
None but the Strong. Bradley, V.
NORTH POLE
  Ross, L. Where There Is No North
North Pole Confidential. Jensen, S.
NORWAY
  Mahlmann, L. Three Billy Goats Gruff
  Nolan, P. The Golden Voice of Little Erik
Nothing Will Battle a Regnant Soul. Bradley, V.
NURSES
  Bradley, V. Sunday at Meadowlake Manor
The Nutcracker Prince. Mahlmann, L.

- O -

O Little Town of Bethlehem. Morley, O.
Oberacker, Shirley. A Christmas Tale. In Kamerman, S. On Stage for Christmas. 18 char

O'Donnell, T. C. The Sandman's Brother. In Jagendorf, M. One-
    Act Plays for Young Folks. 11 char
Off Guard. Bradley, V.
Oh God, My God. Rembrandt, E.
OLD AGE
    Rembrandt, E. And Brings Us to This Season.
Old Ghosts at Home. Murray, J.
Old Glory Grows Up. Miller, H.
Old Kieg of Malfi. Donahue, J.
Old King Cole's Christmas. Atherton, M.
The Old Sleuth. Beck, W.
The Old Woman of the West. Olfson, L.
Olfson, Lewy. A Birthday Anthem for America. In Kamerman, S.
    Patriotic and Historical Plays for Young People. Unspecified
    _____. The Braggart's Clever Wife. In Olfson, L. You Can
    Put on a Show. 7 char
    _____. Christmas Coast to Coast. In Kamerman, S. On Stage
    for Christmas. 13 char
    _____. The Old Woman of the West. In Olfson, L. You Can Put
    on a Show. 3 char
    _____. The Princess Who Was Ten Feet Tall. In Olfson, L.
    You Can Put on a Show. 2 char
    _____. Sing a Song of Holidays! In Kamerman, S. Patriotic
    and Historical Plays for Young People. Unspecified
Once in a Hundred Years. Jagendorf, M.
One, Two, Three! Alexander, S.
The Open Window. Saki
Opening Night. Murray, J.
OPERA
    Korty, C. Opera Singer
Opera Singer. Korty, C.
ORPHANS
    Bailey, A. The Christmas Visitor
    Boiko, C. The Christmas Revel
Our Great Declaration. Fisher, A.
Our Sister, Sitya. Nolan, P.
Owen, Dilys. The Easter Lily. In Owen, D. Play-Games. 9 char
    _____. Follow the Leader. In Owen, D. Play-Games. 7+ char
    _____. The Green Stone. In Owen, D. Play-Games. 11 char
    _____. Horray for the Cup. In Owen, D. Play-Games. 22 char
    _____. In Search of Christmas. In Owen, D. Play-Games. 10
    char
    _____. Indian Country. In Owen, D. Play-Games. 12+ char
    _____. The Magic Peacock. In Owen, D. Play-Games. 7 char
    _____. Pirate Gold. In Owen, D. Play-Games. 14+ char

- P -

Pacca, the Little Bowman. Winther, B.
Paddington Goes to the Hospital. Bradley, A.

_____. Violets for Christmas. <u>In</u> Kamerman, S. A Treasury of
Christmas Songs. 5 char
Piccola. Bennett, R.
The Pied Piper of Hamelin. Mahlmann, L.
PIGS
Mahlmann, L. The Three Little Pigs
The Pilgrim Painting. Rawls, J.
PILGRIMS
Fisher, A. Sing the Songs of Thanksgiving
Rawls, J. The Pilgrim Painting
Young, S. Ship Forever Sailing
Pinocchio and the Fire-Eater. Collodi, C.
Pinocchio and the Fire-Eater. Harris, A.
PIONEERS
Fisher, A. Sing, America, Sing
Pirate Gold. Owen, D.
PIRATES
Bradley, V. Shoes and Ships and a Mermaid
_____. The Story of John Worthington Snee
Owen, D. Hooray for the Cup
_____. Pirate Gold
PITCHER, MOLLY
Boiko, C. The Petticoat Revolution
Fisher, A. "Molly Pitcher"
Hall, M. Molly Pitcher Meets the General
PLANETS
Boiko, C. Escape to the Blue Planet
_____. Take Me to Your Marshal
Gerrold, D. The Trouble with Tribbles
Lane, M. Is There Life on Other Planets?
Moessenger, B. Man in the Red Suit
Murray, J. Visitor from Outer Space
Shore, M. Catastrophe Clarence
PLAY WITHIN A PLAY
Harris, A. Pinocchio and the Fire-Eater
Willment, F. The Whites of Their Eyes
POCAHONTAS
Ross, L. Pocahontas and Captain John Smith
Pocahontas and Captain John Smith. Ross, L.
Poe, Edgar A. The Cask of Amontillado. <u>In</u> Gilfond, H. Walker
Plays for Reading. 4 char
POETRY
Bolt, C. My Best Friend Is 12 Feet High
Bradley, V. Mrs. Clopsaddle Presents Spring
Henderson, N. Casey at the Bat
McGowan, J. The Santa Claus Twins
Maloney, L. I Didn't Know That!
POLAND
Nolan, P. Stanislaw and the Wolf
POLICE
Fisher, A. When Freedom Was News

Traditional. Punch and Judy
POLLUTION
       Deverell, R. The Copetown City Kite Crisis
       Shore, M. Catastrophe Clarence
Popcorn Whoppers. Henderson, N.
The Pot of Gold. McCaslin, N.
Potter, Beatrix. Tale of Peter Rabbit. In Mahlmann, L. and D.
    Jones. Puppet Plays from Favorite Stories. 12 char
POVERTY
       Bradley, V. Apples for Sale
       Fisher, A. Mr. Scrooge Finds Christmas
       Harris, A. Rags to Riches
       Miller, H. The Birds' Christmas Carol
       Morley, O. Little Women
       Olfson, L. Nine Times Christmas
       Wilson, E. The Least of These
PRIDE
       Carlson, B. So Proud
       Lynch-Watson, J. The Emperor's New Clothes
       Mahlmann, L. Beauty and the Beast
       Olfson, L. The Braggart's Clever Wife
       Ringwood, G. The Magic Carpets of Antonio Angelini
Prince Rama. Winther, B.
PRINCES AND PRINCESSES
       Bradley, V. Nester the Jester
       Chorpenning, C. The Sleeping Beauty
       DeRegniers, B. The Mysterious Stranger
       Harris, A. Ming Lee and the Magic Tree
       Mahlmann, L. Aladdin, or The Wonderful Lamp
       _____. Beauty and the Beast
       _____. Cinderella
       _____. Manora, the Bird Princess
       _____. Rapunzel's Tower
       _____. Sleeping Beauty
       _____. Snow White and Rose Red
       _____. Toads and Diamonds
       Majeski, B. Whatever Happened to Good Old Ebenezer
    Scrooge?
       Murray, J. The Greatest Christmas Gift
       Nolan, P. Our Sister, Sitya
       Olfson, L. The Princess Who Was Ten Feet Tall
       Owen, D. The Green Stone
       _____. The Magic Peacock
       Rockwell, T. AIIIEEEEEEEEEE!
       Walker, S. The Birthday of the Infanta
       Winther, B. Fire Demon and South Wind
       _____. The Flying Horse Machine
       _____. Pacca, the Little Bowman
       _____. Prince Rama
The Princess Who Was Ten Feet Tall. Olfson, L.
The Printer in Queen Street. Mayr, G.

Priore, Frank V. 1492 Blues. In Kamerman, S. Holiday Plays
    Around the Year. 12 char
Problems! Problems! Carlson, B.
PROPHETS
    Rembrandt, E. Amos, Man from Tekoah
PUBLISHERS
    Mayr, G. The Printer in Queen Street
    Murray, J. Visitor from Outer Space
Pugh, Shirley. In One Basket. In Jennings, C. and A. Harris.
    Plays Children Love. (Play 1--6; Play 2--3; Play 3--4; Play 4--
    6) 19 char
The Pumpkin. Korty, C.
Punch and Judy. Harris, A.
Punch and Judy. Traditional
PUPPET PLAYS
    Bradley, V. Beware of the Glump
    _____. Flat, Flat, Flat
    _____. Shoes and Ships and a Mermaid
    _____. Tillie's Terror
    _____. What Counts at the County Fair
    _____. Women's Lib Comes to the Hill Country
    Carlson, B. The Whole Truth
    Harris, A. Pinocchio and the Fire-Eater
    _____. Punch and Judy
    Guay, G. The Bling Said Hello
    Mahlmann, L. Aesop's Fables
    _____. Aladdin, or The Wonderful Lamp
    _____. Ali Baba and the Forty Thieves
    _____. Anansi and the Box of Stories
    _____. Baba Yaga
    _____. Beauty and the Beast
    _____. The Blue Willow
    _____. Cinderella
    _____. The Elephant's Child
    _____. The Emperor's Nightingale
    _____. The Gingerbread Boy
    _____. King Midas and the Golden Touch
    _____. King of the Golden River
    _____. The Legend of Urashima
    _____. The Little Indian Brave
    _____. Manora, the Bird Princess
    _____. The Nutcracker Prince
    _____. Perez and Martina
    _____. The Pied Piper of Hamelin
    _____. Puss in Boots
    _____. The Rabbit Who Wanted Red Wings
    _____. Rapunzel's Tower
    _____. Rumpelstiltskin
    _____. Sleeping Beauty
    _____. Snow White and Rose Red
    _____. The Table, the Donkey and the Stick

Murray, J.   The Highway Restaurant
REVENGE
    Gilfond, H.   The Cask of Amontillado
    Mahlmann, L.   The Pied Piper of Hamelin
REVERE, PAUL
    Dias, E.   Horse Sense
    Kane, E.   Paul Revere of Boston
    Mayr, G.   Paul Revere, Rider to Lexington
REVOLUTIONARY WAR (AMERICAN)
    Barbee, L.   A Guide for George Washington
    Bennett, R.   Victory Ball
    Boiko, C.   The Petticoat Revolution
    Brown, A.   The Lantern
    Dias, E.   Horse Sense
    _____.   Martha Washington's Spy
    DuBois, G.   The End of the Road
    Fisher, A.   A Dish of Green Peas
    _____.   "Molly Pitcher"
    _____.   Our Great Declaration
    _____.   A Star for Old Glory
    _____.   Washington Marches On
    _____.   Yankee Doodle Dandy
    Grinins, T.   To Test the Truth
    Hackett, W.   Incident at Valley Forge
    Hall, M.   Molly Pitcher Meets the General
    Hark, M.   Author of Liberty
    Kane, E.   Paul Revere of Boston
    Leuser, E.   The Christmas Sampler
    Mayr, G.   Paul Revere, Rider to Lexington
    Miller, H.   Old Glory Grows Up
    Phillips, M.   All Because of a Scullery Maid
    Slingluff, M.   Naughty Susan
    Smith, J.   Summer Soldier
    Willment, F.   The Whites of Their Eyes
    Wolman, D.   An Imaginary Trial of George Washington
Rhoecus.   Brown, A. F.
Ringwood, Gwen.   The Magic Carpets of Antonio Angelini.   In
    Anonymous.   Kids Plays.   6 char
The Road to Market.   Korty, C.
Roar!   Said the Lion.   Alexander, S.
ROBIN HOOD
    Mason, T.   Robin Hood: A Story of the Forest
Robin Hood: A Story of the Forest.   Mason, T.
Robin Hood and the Match at Nottingham.   Nolan, P.
ROBOTS
    Creative Dramatics.   Robots for Sale
    Deary, T.   Glorygum
    Newman, D.   The Runaway Robots
    Van Horn, B.   The Hillbillies and the Robots
Robots for Sale.   Creative Dramatics
Rockwell, Thomas.   AIIIEEEEEEEEEE!   In Rockwell, T.   How to Eat
    Fried Worms and Other Plays.   30+ char

- S -

SAILORS
    Deary, T. Adventure Island
ST. PATRICK'S DAY
    Bradley, V. Hibernian Picnic
    Watts, F. The Leprechaun Shoemaker
Saki (H. H. Munro). The Open Window. <u>In</u> Gilfond, H. Walker
   Plays for Reading. 6 char
The Sandman's Brother. O'Donnell, T.
Santa Changes His Mind. Sroda, A.
SANTA CLAUS
    Bauman, A. Santa's Alphabet
    Bennett, R. Piccola
    Boiko, C. We Interrupt This Program...
    Bradley, V. If You Recognize Me, Don't Admit It
    Chernak, S. A Visit from St. Nicholas
    Hark, M. Merry Christmas Customs
    _____. What, No Santa Claus?
    Hoppenstedt, E. Santa Goes Mod
    Jensen, S. North Pole Confidential
    Marshall, S. The Year Santa Forgot Christmas
    Martens, A. Santa Claus Is Twins
    McGowan, J. Santa Claus for President
    _____. The Santa Claus Twins
    McSweeny, M. Listen to the Peace and Goodwill
    Miller, H. The Left-Over Reindeer
    _____. Monsieur Santa Claus
    Miller, P. Christmas at the O.K. Corral
    Moessenger, B. Man in the Red Suit
    Moessinger, W. He Won't Be Home for Christmas
    Newman, D. The Christmas Question
    Nicholson, J. Holiday for Santa
    Nolan, P. The Trouble with Christmas
    Phillips, M. Violets for Christmas
    Spamer, C. Twinkle
    Urban, C. Mrs. Claus' Christmas Present
Santa Claus for President. McGowan, J.
Santa Claus Is Twins. Martens, A.
The Santa Claus Twins. McGowan, J.
Santa Goes Mod. Hoppenstedt, E.
Santa! Please Get Up. McSweeny, M.
Santa's Alphabet. Bauman, A.
SATIRE
    Winther, B. Japanese Trio
SATURN
    Murray, J. Space Flight to Saturn
SCHOOL
    Murray, J. First Day at School
SCIENCE
    Bradley, V. Flat, Flat, Flat
SCIENCE FICTION
    Anderson, R. Panic in Space

SHADOWS
     Brown, A. The Little Shadows
SHAKESPEARE, WILLIAM
     Boiko, C. The Christmas Revel
Shavuot. Gabriel, M.
Shaw, Richard. Sleeping Beauty. In Donahue, J. and L. Walsh.
    Five Plays from the Children's Theatre Company of Minneapolis.
    17+ char
Ship Forever Sailing. Young, S.
Shipley, Joseph. Mother Goose Drops In. In Jagendorf, M. One-
    Act Plays for Young Folks. 3 char
SHIPS
     Deary, T. Adventure Island
     Gilfond, H. Shipwreck
Shipwreck. Gilfond, H.
The Shoemaker and the Elves. Very, A.
SHOEMAKERS
     Very, A. The Shoemaker and the Elves
     Wilson, E. The Least of These
SHOES
     Korty, C. Jogging
     Very, A. The Shoemaker and the Elves
Shoes and Ships and a Mermaid. Bradley, V.
SHOPPING
     Bradley, V. Repeat After Me
Shore, Maxine. Catastrophe Clarence. In Kamerman, S. Space and
    Science Fiction Plays for Young People. 6 char
SIAM
     Mahlmann, L. Manora, the Bird Princess
Silent Night. Crichton, M.
The Sing-a-Song Man. Comfort, F.
Sing a Song of Holidays! Olfson, L.
Sing, America, Sing. Fisher, A.
Sing the Songs of Christmas. Fisher, A.
Sing the Songs of Thanksgiving. Fisher, A.
SISTERS
     Hackett, W. A Merry Christmas
     Morley, O. Little Women
The Sixth Juror. Murray, J.
The Skill of Pericles. Nolan, P.
SKITS
     Bradley, V. Apples for Sale
     _____. Better Luck Tomorrow, Mr. Washington
     _____. Don't Fall Asleep, Coach, You Might Possibly
    Dream
     _____. Gwendolyn Gloria Gertrude McFee
     _____. Herlock Sholmes
     _____. How Did We Manage Before the Postman Came?
     _____. If the Rabbit Pickets, You're Doing Something
    Wrong
     _____. Nester the Jester

_____. The Story of John Worthington Snee
_____. Turkeys Take a Dim View of Thanksgiving
_____. You Can't Blame Women for Coming Out of the
    Kitchen
Carlson, B. Belling the Cat
_____. A Pearl in the Barnyard
_____. Rain or Shine
_____. Think Twice
_____. Together or Alone?
_____. The Whole Truth
_____. Who's Stronger?
Lane, M. Is There Life on Other Planets?
SLAVERY
    Harris, A. Androcles and the Lion
    _____. Steal Away Home
    Ross, L. Harriet Tubman, Conductor of the Freedom Train
    Watson, W. Abe and the Runaways
SLEEP
    Chorpenning, C. The Sleeping Beauty
    Comfort, F. The Sing-a-Song Man
    Gilfond, H. David Swan
    Mahlmann, L. Sleeping Beauty
    O'Donnell, T. The Sandman's Brother
    Shaw, R. Sleeping Beauty
The Sleeping Beauty. Chorpenning, C.
Sleeping Beauty. Mahlmann, L.
Sleeping Beauty. Shaw, R.
Slingluff, Mary O. Naughty Susan. In Kamerman, S. Patriotic
    and Historical Plays for Young People. 7 char
Smith, Betty. The Boy, Abe. In Kamerman, S. Holiday Plays
    Around the Year. 12 char
Smith, Jacqueline. Summer Soldier. In Kamerman, S. Patriotic
    and Historical Plays for Young People. 15+ char
SMITH, JOHN
    Ross, L. Pocahontas and Captain John Smith
SNAKES
    Korty, C. The Man Who Loved to Laugh
    Mahlmann, L. The Elephant's Child
    _____. Manora, the Bird Princess
    Winther, B. The Maharajah Is Bored
SNOBBERY
    Boiko, C. The Christmas Revel
    Deary, T. The King of Tarantulus
    Dias, E. Christmas Spirit
Snow White and Rose Red. Mahlmann, L.
Snow White and the Seven Dwarfs. White, J.
So Proud. Carlson, B.
So Young to Die: The Story of Hannah Senesh. Rembrandt, E.
SOLDIERS
    Fisher, A. A Dish of Green Peas
    _____. "Molly Pitcher"

_____. Sing, America, Sing
_____. Yankee Doodle Dandy
Something Scary. Alexander, S.
The Son of William Tell. Nolan, P.
SONGS
     Bradley, V. Amateur Night at Cucumber Center
     _____. Mrs. Clopsaddle Presents Christmas
     Donahue, J. Old Kieg of Malfi
     Fisher, A. Yankee Doodle Dandy
     Korty, C. The Turtle Who Wanted to Fly
     Mahlmann, L. The Emperor's Nightingale
     Martin, J. Everybody, Everybody
     Winther, B. Al Wing Fu and the Golden Dragon
Soul Force. Henderson, N.
SPACE
     Anderson, R. Panic in Space
     Boiko, C. The Book That Saved the Earth
SPACE FANTASY
     Boiko, C. Escape to the Blue Planet
SPACE FLIGHT
     Anderson, R. Panic in Space
     Bauman, A. Close Encounter of a Weird Kind
     Boiko, C. Take Me to Your Marshal
     Fontaine, R. Next Stop, Saturn
     Gerrold, D. The Trouble with Tribbles
     Korty, C. Moon Shot
     Murray, J. Space Flight to Saturn
     _____. Visitor from Outer Space
Space Flight to Saturn. Murray, J.
Space Suit with Roses. Garver, J.
SPAIN
     Nolan, P. The Magic of Salamanca
Spamer, Claribel. Twinkle. In Kamerman, Sylvia. A Treasury of
   Christmas Plays. 7+ char
SPIDERS
     Dias, E. Martha Washington's Spy
     Fisher, A. A Dish of Green Peas
     Korty, C. Ananse's Trick Does Double Work
     Phillips, M. All Because of a Scullery Maid
     Winther, B. Anansi, the African Spider
The Spirit of Sukkot. Gabriel, M.
SPRING
     Alexander, S. Roar! Said the Lion
     Bradley, V. Mrs. Clopsaddle Presents Spring
     Campbell, P. Chinook
     Cavannah, F. Mr. Bunny's Prize
     Henderson, N. Legend for Our Time
Sroda, Anne. Santa Changes His Mind. In Kamerman, S. On Stage
   for Christmas. 5 char
Stanislaw and the Wolf. Nolan, P.
A Star for Old Glory. Fisher, A.

Star of Bethlehem. Martens, A.
Star Over Bethlehem. DuBois, G.
STARS
      Spamer, C. Twinkle
Steal Away Home. Harris, A.
Step on a Crack. Zeder, S.
Stockton, Frank. The Lady or the Tiger. In Gilfond, H. Walker
    Plays for Reading. 8 char
Stokes, Jack. Wiley and the Hairy Man. In Jennings, C. and A.
    Harris. Plays Children Love (A Treasury of Contemporary and
    Classic Plays for Children). 4 char
Stone Soup. McCaslin, N.
The Story of John Worthington Snee. Bradley, V.
STORYTELLING
      Bolt, C. My Best Friend Is 12 Feet High
      Bradley, V. Torko the Terrible
      Carlson, B. Rain or Shine
      Gilfond, H. The Open Window
      Winther, B. The Great Samurai Sword
      _____. Japanese Trio
      _____. Listen to the Hodja
      _____. Prince Rama
Stranger in the Land; The Story of Ruth. Rembrandt, E.
STRENGTH
      Winther, B. Pacca, the Little Bowman
Stretch the Bench. Korty, C.
Strictly Puritan. Miller, H.
STUDENTS
      Martin, J. That's Good, That's Good
Summer Soldier. Smith, J.
Sunday at Meadowlake Manor. Bradley, V.
The Super-Duper Market. Murray, J.
Super Village. Deary, T.
SUPERNATURAL
      Alexander, S. Whatever Happened to Uncle Albert?
SUPERSTITION
      Winther, B. Japanese Trio
Surprise. Bradley, V.
SURVIVAL
      Bradley, V. Arizona Pilgrims
      Deary, T. Super Village
      Donahue, J. How Could You Tell
SUSPENSE
      Holbrook, M. The Toymaker's Doll
      Rockwell, T. The Heiress, or The Croak of Doom
SWEDEN
      Nolan, P. The Gates of Dinkelsbuehl
SWITZERLAND
      Nolan, P. The Son of William Tell
Swortzell, Lowell. The Fisherman and His Wife. In Jennings, C.
    and A. Harris. Plays Children Love. 6+ char

_____. The Fisherman and His Wife. In McCaslin, N. Puppet
    Fun. 3 char

- T -

The Table, the Donkey, and the Stick. Mahlmann, L.
TAILORS
        Jagendorf, M. Bumbo and Scrumbo and Blinko
        Lynch-Watson, J. The Emperor's New Clothes
        Mahlmann, L. The Table, the Donkey and the Stick
        Winther, B. The Maharajah Is Bored
Take Me to Your Marshal. Boiko, C.
The Tale of Lag B'Omer. Gabriel, M.
The Tale of Oniroku. Kraus, J.
Tale of Peter Rabbit. Mahlmann, L.
Tale of Peter Rabbit. Potter, B.
TALENT SHOWS
        Bradley, V. Amateur Night at Cucumber Center
The Talking Cat. McCaslin, N.
The Talking Christmas Tree. Fawcett, M.
TALL TALES
        Henderson, N. Popcorn Whoppers
        Winther, B. John Henry
TEACHERS
        Gaines, F. The Legend of Sleepy Hollow
        Martin, J. That's Good, That's Good
TEENAGERS
        Bradley, V. At the Saturday Matinee
        _____. Nothing Will Rattle a Regnant Soul
        Murray, J. No Experience
TEETH
        Bradley, A. Paddington Visits the Dentist
TELEPHONES
        Bradley, V. Repeat After Me
TELEVISION
        Gabriel, M. This Is Your Life, Israel
        Hoppenstedt, E. Santa Goes Mod
        Majeski, B. Whatever Happened to Good Old Ebenezer
            Scrooge?
        McGowan, J. Bunnies and Bonnets
THAILAND
        Winther, B. White Elephant
THANKSGIVING
        Alexander, S. Meow! and Arf!
        Bradley, V. Arizona Pilgrims
        _____. Turkeys Take a Dim View of Thanksgiving
        DuBois, G. Every Day Is Thanksgiving
        Fisher, A. Sing the Songs of Thanksgiving
        MIller, H. Mr. Snow White's Thanksgiving
        _____. Strictly Puritan

Rawls, J. The Pilgrim Painting
Rembrandt, E. And Brings Us to This Season
Young, S. Ship Forever Sailing
That's Good, That's Good. Martin, J.
Thayer, Ernest. Casey at the Bat. In Henderson, N. Celebrate
America: A Baker's Dozen of Plays. 9+ char
THEATER
Murray, J. The Final Curtain
THIEVES
Bradley, A. Paddington Turns Detective
Carlson, B. So Proud
_____. Who Would Steal a Penny?
Gilfond, H. The Upheaval
Korty, C. Bag of Gold
Mahlmann, L. Ali Baba and the Forty Thieves
Murray, J. I Want to Report a Murder
Nolan, P. Boshibari and the Two Thieves
_____. Robin Hood and the Match at Nottingham
Owen, D. Hooray for the Cup
Winther, B. Abu Nuwas
_____. Japanese Trio
_____. The Monkey Without a Tail
_____. Pacca, the Little Bowman
Think Twice. Carlson, B.
This Is Your Life, Israel. Gabriel, M.
Three Billy Goats Gruff. Mahlmann, L.
Three Little Kittens' Christmas. Christmas, J.
The Three Little Pigs. Mahlmann, L.
Thurston, Cheryl M. and Patsy Miller. Christmas at the O.K. Cor-
ral. In Kamerman, S. Holiday Plays Around the Year. 10+
char
Thurston, Muriel B. Room for Mary. In Kamerman, S. A Treasury
of Christmas Plays. 6 char
The Tiger, the Brahman, and the Jackal. Carlson, B.
Tillie's Terror. Bradley, V.
TIME
Bradley, V. How Did We Manage Before the Postman Came?
Tisha Blav. Gabriel, M.
To Test the Truth. Grinins, T.
Toads and Diamonds. Mahlmann, L.
A Toby Show. Harris, A.
Together or Alone? Carlson, B.
Tolstoy, Leo. Little Girls Wiser Than Men. In Gilfond, H. Walker
Plays for Reading. 12 char
Tom Sawyer. Spencer, S.
Torko the Terrible. Bradley, V.
Touchstone. Runnette, H.
TOURISTS
Bradley, V. Better Luck Tomorrow, Mr. Washington
The Toymaker's Doll. Holbrook, M.
TOYS
Bradley, V. Torko the Terrible.

Hark, M. What, No Santa Claus?
Holbrook, M. The Toymaker's Doll
Mills, G. Christmas Comes to Hamelin
Owen, D. In Search of Christmas
Thane, A. The Christmas Nutcracker
Winther, B. The Villain and the Toy Shop
Traditional Punch and Judy. In Jennings, C. and A. Harris. Plays
    Children Love. 8 char
TRAGEDY
    Bradley, V. The Last Bus from Lockerbee
TRAINS
    Bradley, A. The Arrival of Paddington
The Transfiguration of the Gifts. Cavanah, F.
TREASURE
    Bradley, V. Five Times Sue Is Julia Bates
TREES
    Gabriel, M. Little Tree Learns a Lesson
    _____. The Tale of Lag B'Omer
    Harris, A. Yankee Doodle Dandies
    Martin, J. Big Burger
    Olfson, L. Christmas Coast to Coast
The Trial of Peter Zenger. Nolan, P.
TRIALS
    Alexander, S. The Case of the Kidnapped Nephew
    Gilfond, H. The Lady or the Tiger
    Murray, J. The Sixth Juror
    Nolan, P. The Trial of Peter Zenger
    Spencer, S. Tom Sawyer
    Wolman, D. An Imaginary Trial of George Washington
TRICKERY
    Beck, W. The Estabrook Nieces
    _____. False Pretenses
    Bradley, V. The Haunted House
    _____. Off Guard
    Carlson, B. The Heart of a Monkey
    Gaines, F. The Legend of Sleepy Hollow
    Harris, A. Peck's Bad Boy
    Korty, C. Ananse's Trick Does Double Work
    _____. Clever Clyde
    _____. Mr. Hare Takes Mr. Leopard for a Ride
    Lynch-Watson, J. The Emperor's New Clothes
    Mahlmann, L. Ali Baba and the Forty Thieves
    _____. Anansi and the Box of Stories
    _____. Puss in Boots
    _____. Uncle Remus Tales
    McCaslin, N. Stone Soup
    Nolan, P. Boshibari and the Two Thieves
    _____. The French Cabinetmaker
    Spencer, S. Tom Sawyer
    Stokes, J. Wiley and the Hairy Man
    Wheetley, K. The Buffalo and the Bell

Winther, B.   African Trio
_____.   Anansi, the African Spider
_____.   Ijapa, the Tortoise
_____.   Little Mouse-Deer
_____.   The Monkey Without a Tail
Tricky Gifts.   Alexander, S.
TROLLS
Bradley, V.   Ludlillian and the Dark Road
Mahlmann, L.   Three Billy Goats Gruff
The Trouble with Christmas.   Nolan, P.
The Trouble with Tribbles.   Gerrold, D.
TRUTH AND FALSEHOOD
Crew, H.   The Password
TUBMAN, HARRIET
Harris, A.   Yankee Doodle Dandies
TURKEY
Winther, B.   Listen to the Hodja
Turkeys Take a Dim View of Thanksgiving.   Bradley, V.
The Turtle Who Wanted to Fly.   Korty, C.
Twain, Mark.   The Celebrated Jumping Frog of Calaveras County.
In Gilfond, H.   Walker Plays for Reading.   6 char
_____.   Tom Sawyer.   In Jennings, C. and A. Harris.   Plays
Children Love.   20 char
'Twas the Night Before Christmas.   Pendleton, E.
The Twelve Days of Christmas.   Wright, D.
TWINS
Martens, A.   Santa Claus Is Twins
Two Dilemma Tales.   Winther, B.

- U -

UFO'S
Watts, F.   High Fashion from Mars
Uncle Remus Tales.   Mahlmann, L.
UNDERGROUND RAILROAD
Ross, L.   Harriet, Tubman, Conductor of the Freedom Train
UNITED STATES
Harris, A.   Yankee Doodle Dandies
Mahlmann, L.   The Little Indian Brave
_____.   The Rabbit Who Wanted Red Wings
_____.   Uncle Remus Tales
Stokes, J.   Wiley and the Hairy Man
UNITED STATES--HISTORY
Barbee, L.   The Boston Tea Party
_____.   A Guide for George Washington
Boiko, C.   The Petticoat Revolution
Brown, C.   The Constitution Is Born
Dias, E.   Horse Sense
_____.   Martha Washington's Spy
Fisher, A.   Ask Mr. Jefferson

_____. A Dish of Green Peas
_____. "Molly Pitcher"
_____. Our Great Declaration
_____. Sing, America, Sing
_____. A Star for Old Glory
_____. Washington Marches On
_____. When Freedom Was News
_____. Yankee Doodle Dandy
Grinins, T. To Test the Truth
Hackett, W. Incident at Valley Forge
Hall, M. Molly Pitcher Meets the General
Hark, M. Author of Liberty
Harris, A. Yankee Doodle
Kane, E. Paul Revere of Boston
Marra, D. "Woof" for the Red, White and Blue
Miller, H. Old Glory Grows Up
Nolan, P. The Trial of Peter Zenger
Olfson, L. A Birthday Anthem for America
Phillips, M. All Because of a Scullery Maid
Ross, L. The Boston Tea Party
_____. Pocahontas and Captain John Smith
Slingluff, M. Naughty Susan
Smith, J. Summer Soldier
Willment, F. The Whites of Their Eyes
Wolman, D. An Imaginary Trial of George Washington
Up a Christmas Tree. Fisher, A.
The Upheaval. Gilfond, H.
Urban, Catherine. Mrs. Claus' Christmas Present. In Kamerman, S.
   A Treasury of Christmas Plays. 6 char

- V -

VALENTINE'S DAY
   Alexander, S. Good Day, Giant!
   Bradley, V. The Big Red Heart
   Callanan, C. Cupid and Company
   McGowan, J. Miss Lonelyheart
Van Horn, Bill. The Hillbillies and the Robots. In Kamerman, S.
   Space and Science Fiction Plays for Young People. 18+ char
VANITY
   Abisch, R. Mrs. Snooty and the Waiter
   Lynch-Watson, J. The Emperor's New Clothes
   Walker, S. The Birthday of the Infanta
VARIETY PROGRAMS
   Bradley, V. Amateur Night at Cucumber Center
   _____. Mrs. Clopsaddle Presents Christmas
VAUDEVILLE
   Harris, A. A Toby Show
VENTRILOQUISM
   Murray, J. I Want to Report a Murder

VERSE PLAYS
     Barbee, L. A Guide for George Washington
Victory Ball. Bennett, R.
VIETNAM
     Winther, B. Follow the River Lai
VIETNAM WAR
     Henderson, N. Honor the Brave
VILLAGES
     Carlson, B. Crowded?
     _____. Problems! Problems!
     Nolan, P. Licha's Birthday Serenade
The Villain and the Toy Shop. Winther, B.
VILLAINS
     Bradley, V. The Haunted House
     _____. Tillie's Terror
     Winther, B. The Villain and the Toy Shop
Violets for Christmas. Phillips, M.
Visions of Sugar Plums. Marlens, A.
A Visit from St. Nicholas. Chermak, S.
Visiting Hours. Murray, J.
Visitor from Outer Space. Murray, J.

- W -

Waite, Helen and Elbert Hoppenstedt. The Master of the Strait. In
    Kamerman, S. A Treasury of Christmas Plays. 7 char
Walk-Up on Christopher. Bradley, V.
Walker, Stuart. The Birthday of the Infanta. In Jennings, C. and
    A. Harris. Plays Children Love. 7 char
WAR
     Fisher, A. Sing, America, Sing
     Henderson, N. Honor the Brave
     Nolan, P. The Gates of Dinkelsbuehl
Warren, Lee. The Palmwine Drinkard. In Warren, L. The Theater
    of Africa; An Introduction. 3 char
    _____. Woyengi. In Warren, L. The Theater of Africa; An In-
    troduction. 6+ char
WASHINGTON, GEORGE
     Barbee, L. A Guide for George Washington
     Bennett, R. Victory Ball
     Bradley, V. Better Luck Tomorrow, Mr. Washington
     _____. Miss Lacey and the President
     Dias, E. Martha Washington's Spy
     DuBois, G. The End of the Road
     Fisher, A. A Dish of Green Peas
     _____. George Washington, Farmer
     _____. Washington Marches On
     Grinins, T. To Test the Truth
     Hall, M. Molly Pitcher Meets the General
     Miller, H. Old Glory Grows Up

Washington Marches On. Fisher, A.
WASHINGTON, MARTHA
      Boiko, C. The Petticoat Revolution
      Bradley, V. Better Luck Tomorrow, Mr. Washington
      Dias, E. Martha Washington's Spy
      Fisher, A. Washington Marches On
      Hackett, W. Incident at Valley Forge
WASHINGTON'S BIRTHDAY
      Bradley, V. Miss Lacey and the President
      DuBois, G. The End of the Road
      Pendleton, E. Let George Do It
Watkins, Martha S. Nobody Believes in Witches. In Kamerman, S.
    Holiday Plays Around the Year. 6 char
Watson, Wenta Jean. Abe and the Runaways. In Kamerman, S.
    Holiday Plays Around the Year. 11 char
Watts, Frances B. High Fashion from Mars. In Kamerman, S.
    Space and Science Fiction Plays for Young People. 10 char
    _____. The Leprechaun Shoemaker. In Kamerman, S. Holiday
    Plays Around the Year. 12+ char
The Way. Runnette, H.
We Interrupt This Program... Boiko, C.
WEDDINGS
      Murray, J. Mother of the Bride
WEREWOLVES
      Alexander, S. Whatever Happened to Uncle Albert?
THE WEST
      Deary, T. The Custard Kid
      Miller, P. Christmas at the O.K. Corral
What Counts at the County Fair. Bradley, V.
What Kind of Hat? Abisch, R.
What, No Santa Claus? Hark, M. and N. McQueen
What Took You So Long? Bradley, V.
What Will You Tell Us of Christmas? Bradley, V.
Whatever Happened to Good Old Ebenezer Scrooge? Majeski, B.
Whatever Happened to Uncle Albert? Alexander, S.
Wheetley, Kim. The Buffalo and the Bell. In Jennings, C. and
    A. Harris. Plays Children Love. 8+ char
When Freedom Was News. Fisher, A.
Where Love Is, There God Is Also. Tolstoi, L. (Play title: The
    Least of These written by Wilson, E. and Anna Field)
Where There Is No North. Ross, L.
Which Is Witch? Rostetter, A.
White, Jessie. Snow White and the Seven Dwarfs. In Jennings, C.
    and A. Harris. Plays Children Love. 23 char
A White Christmas. Barr, J.
White Elephant. Winther, B.
The Whites of Their Eyes. Willment, F.
Who Would Steal a Penny? Carlson, B.
The Whole Truth. Carlson, B.
Who's Stronger? Carlson, B.
Wiggins, Kate Douglas. The Birds' Christmas Carol. In Kamerman,
    S. Christmas Play Favorites for Young People. 18+ char

Wiley and the Hairy Man. Stokes, J.
Willment, Frank. The Whites of Their Eyes. In Kamerman, S.
    Patriotic and Historical Plays for Young People. 19 char
Wilson, Ella and Anna Field. The Least of These. In McSweeny,
    M. Christmas Plays for Young Players. 8+ char
WIND
      Barr, J. A White Christmas
      Carlson, B. Who's Stronger?
      Janney, S. The East Wind's Revenge
      Mahlmann, L. King of the Golden River
      Martin, J. Blown Off the Billboard
      McGowan, J. The Coming of the Prince
      Winther, B. Fire Demon and South Wind
Winnie-the-Pooh. Sergel, K.
WINTER
      Bradley, V. The Night That Time Sat Still
      Campbell, P. Chinook
      Nolan, P. The Double Nine of Chih Yuan
Winther, Barbara. Abu Nuwas. In Winther, B. Plays from Folk-
    tales of Africa and Asia. (Story 1--8 char; Story 2--8 char)
_____. African Trio. In Winther, B. Plays from Folktales of
    Africa and Asia. (Story 1--10 char; Story 2--9+ char; Story 3--
    9 char)
_____. Ah Wing Fu and the Golden Dragon. In Winther, B.
    Plays from Folktales of Africa and Asia. 14 char
_____. Anansi, the African Spider. In Winther, B. Plays from
    Folktales of Africa and Asia. (Story 1--7 char; Story 2--9
    char; Story 3--7 char)
_____. Bata's Lessons. In Winther, B. Plays from Folktales of
    Africa and Asia. 13 char
_____. Fire Demon and South Wind. In Winther, B. Plays from
    Folktales of Africa and Asia. 13 char
_____. The Flying Horse Machine. In Winther, B. Plays from
    Folktales of Africa and Asia. 9+ char
_____. Follow the River Lai. In Winther, B. Plays from Folk-
    tales of Africa and Asia. 12+ char
_____. The Great Samurai Sword. In Winther, B. Plays from
    Folktales of Africa and Asia. 12 char
_____. Ijapa, the Tortoise. In Winther, B. Plays from Folktales
    of Africa and Asia. (Story 1--8+ char; Story 2--7 char)
_____. Japanese Trio. In Winther, B. Plays from Folktales of
    Africa and Asia. 12 char
_____. John Henry. In Kamerman, S. Holiday Plays Around the
    Year. 10+ char
_____. Listen to the Hodja. In Winther, B. Plays from Folktales
    of Africa and Asia. 12 char
_____. Little Mouse-Deer. In Winther, B. Plays from Folktales
    of Africa and Asia. 12 char
_____. The Maharajah Is Bored. In Jennings, C. and A. Harris.
    Plays Children Love (A Treasury of Contemporary and Classic
    Plays for Children). 10+ char

_____. The Monkey Without a Tail. In Winther, B. Plays from Folktales of Africa and Asia. 7+ char

_____. Pacca, the Little Bowman. In Winther, B. Plays from Folktales of Africa and Asia. 10+ char

_____. Prince Rama. In Winther, B. Plays from Folktales of Africa and Asia. 10+ char

_____. Two Dilemma Tales. In Winther, B. Plays from Folktales of Africa and Asia. (Story 1--6+ char; Story 2--5+ char)

_____. The Villain and the Toy Shop. In Kamerman, S. On Stage for Christmas. 20 char

_____. White Elephant. In Winther, B. White Elephant. 11 char

WISHES

> Brown, A. The Wishing Moon
> Korty, C. The Turtle Who Wanted to Fly
> Mahlmann, L. The Rabbit Who Wanted Red Wings
> Pugh, S. In One Basket

The Wishing Moon. Brown, A.

WITCHES

> Abisch, R. What Kind of Hat?
> Bradley, V. Ludlillian and the Dark Road
> DeRegniers, B. The Mysterious Stranger
> Mahlmann, L. Baba Yaga
> _____. Rapunzel's Tower
> Majeski, B. Whatever Happened to Good Old Ebenezer Scrooge?
> Marks, B. The Beauty Potion
> Miller, H. The Broomstick Beauty
> Murray, J. The Greatest Christmas Gift
> Olfson, L. The Old Woman of the West
> Rostetter, A. Which Is Witch?
> Watkins, M. Nobody Believes in Witches

WIVES

> Bradley, V. Here Lies McClean
> _____. You Can't Blame Women for Coming Out of the Kitchen

WIZARDS

> DeRegniers, B. The Magic Spell

Wolman, Diana. An Imaginary Trial of George Washington. In Kamerman, S. Patriotic and Historical Plays for Young People. 18+ char

WOLVES

> Mahlmann, L. The Three Little Pigs

Women's Lib Comes to the Hill Country. Bradley, V.

"Woof" for the Red, White, and Blue. Marra, D.

WORLD WAR II

> Rembrandt, E. So Young to Die

WORMS

> Rockwell, T. How to Eat Fried Worms

Woyengi. Warren, L.

Wright, Doris. The Twelve Days of Christmas. In Kamerman, S. A Treasury of Christmas Plays. 78 char

Wright, Rowe. Five Ghosts. In Jagendorf, M. A. One-Act Plays
for Young Folks. 5 char

- Y -

Yankee Doodle. Harris, A.
Yankee Doodle Dandies. Harris, A.
Yankee Doodle Dandy. Fisher, A.
The Year Santa Forgot Christmas. Marshall, S.
You Can't Blame Women for Coming Out of the Kitchen. Bradley, V.
You Can't Win 'Em All. Bradley, V.
You Have to Stay on the Horse. Bradley, V.
Young, Stanley. Ship Forever Sailing. In Kamerman, S. Holiday
Plays Around the Year. 23 char

- Z -

Zedar, Suzan. Step on a Crack. In Jennings, C. and A. Harris.
Plays Children Love. 6 char
ZENGER, PETER
Nolan, P. The Trial of Peter Zenger

CAST ANALYSIS

The following listing is divided into four parts: female cast, male cast, mixed cast, and puppet plays. Under each part, the arrangement is from few to many characters.

FEMALE CAST

1 character

Murray, John. Bargain Day
_____. Den Mother
_____. Do or Diet
_____. The Driving Lesson
_____. First Day at School
_____. The Fish Story
_____. For Art's Sake
_____. The Introduction
_____. Kiddie Matinee
_____. Mother of the Bride
_____. Moving Day
_____. No Experience
_____. Opening Night
_____. Space Flight to Saturn
_____. The Super-Duper Market
_____. Visiting Hours

6 characters

Henderson, Nancy. Little Women
Thurston, Muriel. Room for Mary

7 characters

Fawcett, Margaret. The Talking Christmas Tree

9 characters

Hackett, Walter. A Merry Christmas
Morley, Olive. Little Women

14 characters

Boiko, Claire. The Petticoat Revolution

MALE CAST

1 character

Murray, John. A Case for Two Detectives
_____. Even a Child Can Do It
_____. The Highway Restaurant
_____. Home Movies
_____. Home Sweet Home Computer
_____. It's a Mystery to Me
_____. It's Magic
_____. Model Plane

4 characters

Deary, Terence. Adventure Island
Gilfond, Henry. The Cask of Amontillado

6 characters

Gilfond, Henry. The Celebrated Jumping Frog of Calaveras
    County
Golden, Joseph. Johnny Moonbeam and the Silver Arrow
Shore, Maxine. Catastrophe Clarence

10 characters

Mayr, Grace Alicia. The Printer in Queen Street

12 characters

Nicol, Eric. Beware the Quickly Who

23 characters

Young, Stanley. Ship Forever Sailing

MIXED CAST

2 characters

Abisch, Roz. Mrs. Snooty and the Waiter
_____. What Kind of Hat?
Alexander, Sue. Come Quick!
_____. Good Day, Giant!
_____. Meow! and Arf!
_____. One, Two, Three!
_____. Roar! Said the Lion
_____. Something Scary
_____. Tricky Gifts
Carlson, Bernice. The Heart of a Monkey
Korty, Carol. Jogging

2 characters and extras

Chermak, Sylvia. The Elves and the Shoemaker
Newman, Deborah. The Christmas Question

3 characters

Carlson, Bernice. Think Twice
_____. Who's Stronger?
Korty, Carol. Bag of Gold
_____. The Flagpole
_____. Mr. Hare Takes Mr. Leopard for a Ride
_____. Opera Singer
_____. The Road to Market
_____. The Turtle Who Wanted to Fly

Murray, John. The Door
Nolan, Paul T. Boshibari and the Two Thieves
Warren, Lee. The Palmwine Drinkard
Shipley, Joseph. Mother Goose Drops In

3 characters and extras

Bradley, Virginia. Better Luck Tomorrow, Mr. Washington
_____. None but the Strong
Stokes, Jack. Wiley and the Hairy Man

4 characters

Bradley, Virginia. Apples for Sale
_____. You Can't Blame Women for Coming Out of the
  Kitchen
_____. You Can't Win 'Em All
Brown, Abbie Farwell. Rhoecus
Callanan, Cecelia. Cupid and Company
Carlson, Bernice. So Proud
Deary, Terence. Adventure Island
_____. The Custard Kid
_____. Glorygum
_____. The King of Tarantulus
deMaupassant, Guy. The Necklace
Gilfond, Henry. The Last Leaf
Jagendorf, Moritz. Bumbo and Scrumbo and Blinko
Korty, Carol. The Pumpkin
_____. Stretch the Bench
Martin, Judith. Everybody, Everybody
_____. Hands Off! Don't Touch!
_____. Ma and the Kids
_____. That's Good, That's Good
Ross, Laura. Pocahontas and Captain John Smith

4 characters and extras

Bradley, Virginia. The Greater Miracle
Fisher, Aileen. "Molly Pitcher"
Martin, Judith. The Chicken and the Egg

5 characters

Alexander, Sue. Mystery of the Stone Statues
_____. Whatever Happened to Uncle Albert?
Beck, Warren. Imagination
Bennett, Rowena. Piccola
Bolt, Carol. My Best Friend Is 12 Feet High
Bradley, Alfred. Paddington Goes to the Launderette
Bradley, Virginia. Off Guard
_____. Turkeys Take a Dim View of Thanksgiving
Brown, Abbie Farwell. The Little Shadows
Carlson, Bernice. The Country Mouse and the City Mouse
_____. Rain or Shine
DeRegniers, Beatrice Schenk. The Magic Spell
Deary, Terence. The Factory
Fisher, Aileen. Ask Mr. Jefferson
_____. A Dish of Green Peas
Gilfond, Henry. The Romance of a Busy Broker
Korty, Carol. Ananse's Trick Does Double Work
_____. Building the House
_____. Clever Clyde.
_____. Moon Shot
Maloney, Louis. I Didn't Know That!
Marra, Dorothy Brandt. "Woof" for the Red, White and
    Blue
Martin, Judith. The Building and the Statue
_____. I Won't Take a Bath!
Nolan, Paul T. The Double Nine of Chih Yuan
Pendleton, Edrie. 'Twas the Night Before Christmas
Phillips, Marguerite Kreger. Violets for Christmas
Sroda, Anne. Santa Changes His Mind
Wright, Rowe. Five Ghosts

5 characters and extras

Bradley, Virginia. A Groundhog by Any Other Name...
_____. Surprise
Capell, Loretta Camp. The First Christmas Tree

6 characters

Barbee, Lindsay. A Guide for George Washington
Bradley, Virginia. The Big Red Heart

_____. The Bracelet Engagement
_____. Five Times Sue Is Julia Bates
_____. Walk-Up on Christopher
_____. You Have to Stay on the Horse
Campbell, Paddy. Chinook
Carlson, Bernice. Clever--Eh?
_____. Lion, Sick and Dying
Clapp, Patricia. Christmas in Old New England
Fisher, Aileen. Up a Christmas Tree
Fontaine, Robert. Next Stop, Saturn
Gilfond, Henry. The Open Window
_____. The Upheaval
Harris, Aurand. Androcles and the Lion
Howard, Helen L. Candles for Christmas
Lane, Marion. Is There Life on Other Planets?
Martin, Judith. Big Burger
_____. Blown Off the Billboard
Miller, Helen Louise. The Broomstick Beauty
_____. A Christmas Promise
Murray, John. Dead of Night
Nolan, Paul T. The Courters
_____. The Magic of Salamanca
Pendleton, Edrie. Let George Do It
Peterson, Mary Nygaard. Adobe Christmas
Rafferty, Robert. Jack and the Beanstalk
Ringwood, Gwen. The Magic Carpets of Antonio Angelini
Rostetter, Alice. Which Is Witch?
Urban, Catherine. Mrs. Claus' Christmas Present
Watkins, Martha Swintz. Nobody Believes in Witches
Zeder, Suzan. Step on a Crack.

6 characters and extras

Carlson, Bernice. A Pearl in the Barnyard
Comfort, Florence C. The Sing-a-Song Man
duBois, Graham. Bonds of Affection
Hark, Mildred. Christmas Shopping Early
Warren, Lee. Woyengi
Winther, Barbara. Two Dilemma Tales

6 characters and others

Swortzell, Lowell. The Fisherman and His Wife

7 characters

Alexander, Sue.   The Ghost of Plymouth Castle
Barbee, Lindsay.   The Boston Tea Party
Beck, Warren.   Great Caesar
Boiko, Claire.   The Book That Saved the Earth
Bradley, Alfred.   The Arrival of Paddington
_____ .   Paddington Goes to the Hospital
Bradley, Virginia.   Arizona Pilgrims
_____ .   Here Lies McClean
_____ .   Mrs. Clopsaddle Presents Christmas
Carlson, Bernice.   Crowded?
_____ .   Half of the Reward
Crichton, Madge.   Silent Night
Deverell, Rex.   The Copetown City Kite Crisis
Dias, Earl J.   Horse Sense
_____ .   The Little Man Who Wasn't There
_____ .   Martha Washington's Spy
duBois, Graham.   The End of the Road
Fawcett, Margaret Georgia.   The Talking Christmas Tree
Fisher, Aileen.   A Star for Old Glory
Harris, Aurand.   Peck's Bad Boy
_____ .   A Toby Show
Head, Faye E.   The Second Shepherd's Play
Jagendorf, Moritz.   Once in a Hundred Years
Marlens, Anne Coulter.   Visions of Sugar Plums
Miller, Helen Louise.   Mr. Snow White's Thanksgiving
_____ .   Puppy Love
Nolan, Paul T.   The Trouble with Christmas
Owen, Dilys.   Follow the Leader
_____ .   The Magic Peacock
Slingluff, Mary O.   Naughty Susan
Waite, Helen E.   The Master of the Strait
Walker, Stuart.   The Birthday of the Infanta
Winther, Barbara.   Anansi, the African Spider

7 characters and extras

Bradley, Virginia.   Help!
_____ .   If the Rabbit Pickets, You're Doing Something
   Wrong
_____ .   Ludlillian and the Dark Road
_____ .   What Will You Tell Us of Christmas?
Carlson, Bernice.   Belling the Cat

Creative Dramatics. Robots for Sale
Murray, John. An International Affair
Spamer, Claribel. Twinkle
Winther, Barbara. The Monkey Without a Tail

8 characters

Anderson, Robert. Panic in Space
Bauman, A. F. Close Encounter of a Weird Kind
Beck, Warren. The Estabrook Nieces
Bradley, Alfred. Paddington Has a Birthday
_____. Paddington Paints a Picture
_____. Paddington Visits the Dentist
Bradley, Virginia. Callyope, the Crying Comic
_____. Miss Lacey and the President
_____. Quick! The River's Rising
Carlson, Bernice. Together or Alone?
Chaloner, Gwen. The Bookworm
DeRegniers, Beatrice Schenk. The Mysterious Stranger
Dias, Earl. Christmas Spirit
_____. Christmas Spirit
Gilfond, Henry. The Lady or the Tiger
Hackett, Walter. Incident at Valley Forge
Hall, Marjory. Molly Pitcher Meets the General
Hark, Mildred. Author of Liberty
_____. Christmas Recaptured
McGowan, Jane. Miss Lonelyheart
Murray, John. I Want to Report a Murder
Nolan, Paul T. The French Cabinetmaker
_____. A Leak in the Dike
Phillips, Marguerite Kreger. All Because of a Scullery Maid
Ross, Laura. Harriet Tubman, Conductor of the Freedom
    Train
Very, Alice--adaptor. The Shoemaker and the Elves
Winther, Barbara. Abu Nuwas

8 characters and extras

Bradley, Virginia. Hibernian Picnic
_____. Nothing Will Rattle a Regnant Soul
_____. A Roll of Nickels
Fisher, Aileen. Yankee Doodle Dandy
Wheetley, Kim. The Buffalo and the Bell

Holbrook, Marion. The Toymaker's Doll
Nolan, Paul T. The Gates of Dinkelsbuehl
_____. The Highland Fling
Wilson, Ella. The Least of These
Winther, Barbara. Ijapa, the Tortoise

9 characters

Alexander, Sue. The Case of the Kidnapped Nephew
Bradley, Alfred. Paddington Turns Detective
Bradley, Virginia. Don't Fall Asleep, Coach, You Might
    Possibly Dream
_____. Herlock Sholmes
_____. Repeat After Me
Carlson, Bernice. Anyone Could, But---
_____. Problems! Problems!
_____. Who Would Steal a Penny?
Du Bois, Graham. Every Day Is Thanksgiving
Guay, Georgette. The Bling Said Hello
Jensen, Stanley C. North Pole Confidential
Morley, Olive J. Little Women
Murray, John. Old Ghosts at Home
Nicholson, Jessie. Holiday for Santa
Nolan, Paul T. Johnny Appleseed
_____. Stanislaw and the Wolf
Owen, Dilys. The Easter Lily
Peacock, Mary. Keeping Christmas
Rawls, James. The Pilgrim Painting
Rockwell, Thomas. The Heiress, or The Croak of Doom
Thane, Adele. Christmas Every Day

9 characters and others

Bailey, Anne Howard. The Christmas Visitor

9 characters and extras

Bradley, Virginia. Amateur Night at Cucumber Center
_____. The Haunted House
_____. The Last Bus from Lockerbee
_____. What Took You So Long?
Carlson, Bernice. The Tiger, the Brahman, and the Jackal

Cavanah, Frances. The Transfiguration of the Gifts
Deary, Terence. Super Village
Hark, Mildred. What, No Santa Claus?
Harris, Aurand. Rags to Riches
Henderson, Nancy. Hail the Lucky Year
_____. Little Turtle
_____--adaptor. Casey at the Bat
Martens, Anne Coulter. Santa Claus Is Twins
Murray, John. Airport Adventure
Nolan, Paul T. The Golden Voice of Little Erik
Winther, Barbara. African Trio
_____. The Flying Horse Machine

10 characters

Beck, Warren. The Old Sleuth
Boiko, Claire. Take Me to Your Marshal
Bradley, Virginia. Nester the Jester
_____. The Night That Time Sat Still
Du Bois, Graham. A Room for a King
Duvall, Lucille M. The Chosen One
Fisher, Aileen. When Freedom Was News
Gilfond, Henry. The Duel
_____. Shipwreck
Hark, Mildred. Merry Christmas Customs
_____. Reindeer on the Roof
Henderson, Nancy. "John Muir, Earth-Planet, Universe"
McSweeny, Maxine. Listen to the Peace and Goodwill
Murray, John. The Looking Glass Murder
Ross, Laura. Where There Is No North
Watts, Frances B. High Fashion from Mars

10 characters and extras

Bradley, Virginia. Abe Lincoln: Star Center
_____. At the Saturday Matinee
_____. The Carousel and a Cold Fried Egg
_____. Sunday at Meadowlake Manor
Leuser, Eleanor D. The Christmas Sampler
_____. The Legend of the Christmas Rose
Newman, Deborah. The Runaway Robots
Nolan, Paul T. Robin Hood and the Match at Nottingham
_____. The Skill of Pericles

Rockwell, Thomas. Myron Mere
Traditional. A Christmas Pageant
Winther, Barbara. John Henry
_____. The Maharajah Is Bored
_____. Pacca, the Little Bowman
_____. Prince Rama

11 characters

Beck, Warren. False Pretenses
Boiko, Claire. Escape to the Blue Planet
Cavannah, Frances. Mr. Bunny's Prize
Christms, Joyce S. Three Little Kittens' Christmas
Dias, Earl J. The Christmas Starlet
Janney, Sam. The East Wind's Revenge
Miller, Helen Louise. Season's Greetings
_____. Strictly Puritan
Morley, Olive J. O Little Town of Bethlehem
Nolan, Paul T. The Son of William Tell
O'Donnell, T. C. The Sandman's Brother
Olfson, Lewy--adaptor. Nine Times Christmas
Owen, Dilys. The Green Stone
Watson, Wenta. Abe and the Runaways
Winther, Barbara. White Elephant

11 characters and extras

Atherton, Marguerite. Old King Cole's Christmas
Du Bois, Graham. The Humblest Place
Fisher, Aileen. Sing the Songs of Thanksgiving
Korty, Carol. The Man Who Loved to Laugh
Marshall, Sheila L. The Year Santa Forgot Christmas
Miller, Helen Louise. The Left-Over Reindeer
Murray, John. The Final Curtain

12 characters

Bradley, Virginia. How Did We Manage Before the Postman
    Came?
_____. Mrs. Clopsaddle Presents Spring
Chorpenning, Charlotte B. The Sleeping Beauty
Gilfond, Henry. Little Girls Wiser Than Men

Harris, Aurand. Yankee Doodle
Henderson, Nancy. Legend for Our Time
_____. Popcorn Whoppers
Kraus, Joanna. The Dragon Hammer
_____. The Tale of Oniroku
McSweeny, Maxine. The Christmas Party
Miller, Helen Louise. Red Carpet Christmas
Murray, John. A Case for Two Detectives
Owen, Dilys. Indian Country
Priore, Frank V. 1492 Blues
Smith, Betty. The Boy, Abe
Thane, Adele. The Christmas Nutcracker
Watts, Frances. The Leprechaun Shoemaker
Winther, Barbara. The Great Samurai Sword
_____. Japanese Trio
_____. Listen to the Hodja
_____. Little Mouse-Deer

12 characters and extras

Bennett, Rowena. Granny Goodman's Christmas
DuBois, Graham. Star Over Bethlehem
Fisher, Aileen. Sing, America, Sing
Grinins, Tekla. To Test the Truth
Hoppenstedt, Elbert. Santa Goes Mod
Miller, Patsy and Thurston, Cheryl Miller. Christmas at
    the O.K. Corral
Winther, Barbara. Follow the River Lai

13 characters

Garver, Juliet. Space Suit with Roses
Henderson, Nancy. Moonlife 2069
Olfson, Lewy. Christmas Coast to Coast
Rockwell, Thomas. How to Eat Fried Worms
Winther, Barbara. Bata's Lessons
_____. Fire Demon and South Wind

13 characters and extras

Brown, Abbie Farwell. The Lantern
Gaines, Frederick. The Legend of Sleepy Hollow

Lawler, Lillian.   In the Kitchen of the King
Sergel, Kristin.   Winnie-the-Pooh

14 characters

Brown, Carol J.   The Constitution Is Born
Henderson, Nancy.   The Land We Love
Majeski, Bill.   Whatever Happened to Good Old Ebenezer
    Scrooge?
McSweeny, Maxine.   Santa!   Please Get Up
Nolan, Paul T.   Licha's Birthday Serenade
Winther, Barbara.   Ah Wing Fu and the Golden Dragon

14 characters and extras

Moessenger, Bill.   Man in the Red Suit
Murray, John.   The Greatest Christmas Gift
Owen, Dilys.   Pirate Gold
Patterson, Emma L.   No Room at the Inn

15 characters

Barr, June.   A White Christmas
Carlson, Bernice.   The Law of the Jungle
Farrar, John.   The Garden at the Zoo
Murray, John.   Visitor from Outer Space

15 characters and extras

Crew, Helen.   The Password
McGowan, Jane.   The Santa Claus Twins
_____ .   Bunnies and Bonnets
McQueen, Noel.   Merry Christmas, Crawfords!
Moessinger, William.   He Won't Be Home for Christmas
Smith, Jacqueline V.   Summer Soldier

16 characters

Mayr, Grace Alicia.   Paul Revere, Rider to Lexington
Miller, Helen Louise.   Monsieur Santa Claus

Olfson, Lewy. A Christmas Carol
Owen, Dilys. In Search of Christmas

16 characters and extras

Bradley, Virginia. Torko the Terrible
Murray, John. Flight International
Nolan, Paul T. The Trial of Peter Zenger
Ross, Laura. The Boston Tea Party

17 characters

Kane, Eleanora Bowling. Paul Revere of Boston
McQueen, Noel. Merry Christmas, Crawfords!
Olfson, Lewy. The Birds' Christmas Carol
Purdy, Nina. The Heritage
Runnette, Helen V. The Way

17 characters and extras

Bradley, Virginia. The Story of John Worthington Snee
Harris, Aurand. Ming Lee and the Magic Tree
Shaw, Richard. Sleeping Beauty

18 characters

Gilfond, Henry. David Swan
McGowan, Jane. Santa Claus for President
Oberacker, Shirley C. A Christmas Tale

18 characters and extras

Fisher, Aileen. Mr. Scrooge Finds Christmas
Gerrold, David. The Trouble with Tribbles
Harris, Aurand. Yankee Doodle Dandies
Miller, Helen Louise. The Birds' Christmas Carol
Wolman, Diana. An Imaginary Trial of George Washington

19 characters

Bradley, Virginia. Gwendolyn Gloria Gertrude McFee
Brown, Abbie Farwell. The Wishing Moon
Duvall, Lucille M. Little Chip's Christmas Tree
Kamerman, Sylvia. Nine Cheers for Christmas
Miller, Helen Louise. Old Glory Grows Up
Pugh, Shirley. In One Basket
Willment, Frank. The Whites of Their Eyes

19 characters and extras

Henderson, Nancy. Soul Force
Mason, Timothy. Kidnapped in London

20 characters

Spencer, Sara. Tom Sawyer
Winther, Barbara. The Villain and the Toy Shop

20 characters and extras

Bradley, Virginia. If You Recognize Me, Don't Admit It
Fisher, Aileen. Our Great Declaration

21 characters

Donahue, John. The Cookie Jar

22 characters

Albert, Rollin. A New Angle on Christmas
Chermak, Sylvia. A Visit from St. Nicholas
McGowan, Jane. Christmas Every Day
Owen, Dilys. Hooray for the Cup

22 characters and extras

Murray, John. The Sixth Juror

23 characters

White, Jessie Braham. Snow White and the Seven Dwarfs

23 characters and extras

Harris, Aurand. Steal Away Home
Nolan, Paul T. And Christmas Is Its Name

24 characters

Thane, Adele. A Christmas Carol
Van Horn, Bill. The Hillbillies and the Robots

24 characters and extras

Henderson, Nancy. Come to the Fair
_____. M.D. in Petticoats

25 characters and extras

Donahue, John. Old Kieg of Malfi
Mills, Grace Evelyn. Christmas Comes to Hamelin

26 characters and extras

Martens, Anne Coulter. Star of Bethlehem
Mason, Timothy. Robin Hood: A Story of the Forest

28 characters

Runnette, Helen V. Touchstone

28 characters and extras

McGowan, Jane. The Coming of the Prince

29 characters

Bauman, A. F. Santa's Alphabet

30 characters and extras

Rockwell, Thomas. Aiiieeeeeeeeee!

31 characters and extras

Gaines, Frederick. A Christmas Carol

32 characters

Boiko, Claire. We Interrupt This Program...

33 characters

Fisher, Aileen. Washington Marches On

40 characters

Donahue, John. How Could You Tell

44 characters

Fisher, Aileen. Sing the Songs of Christmas

78 characters

Wright, Doris. The Twelve Days of Christmas

Unspecified

Bennett, Rowena. Victory Ball
Fisher, Aileen. George Washington, Farmer
Olfson, Lewy. A Birthday Anthem for America
_____. Sing a Song of Holidays!

PUPPET PLAYS

1 character

Marks, Burton. The Cooking Lesson
_____. Memory Course

2 characters

Marks, Burton. The Rope
McCaslin, Nellie. George, the Timid Ghost
_____. Little Indian Two Feet's Horse
_____. Stone Soup
Olfson, Lewy. The Princess Who Was Ten Feet Tall

3 characters

Bradley, Virginia. What Counts at the County Fair
Lynch-Watson, Janet. The Lion and the Mouse
Marks, Burton. The Beauty Potion
_____. The Concert
McCaslin, Nellie. The Blacksmith and the Carpenter
_____. The Fisherman and His Wife
_____. The Lantern and the Fan.
_____. The Pot of Gold
Olfson, Lewy. The Old Woman of the West

4 characters

Bradley, Virginia. Women's Lib Comes to the Hill Country
McCaslin, Nellie. The Talking Cat

5 characters

Carlson, Bernice. The Whole Truth
Mahlmann, Lewis. Anansi and the Box of Stories
_____. The 3 Little Pigs

6 characters

Bradley, Virginia. Tillie's Terror
Lynch-Watson, Janet. The Little Red Hen
Mahlmann, Lewis. Rumpelstiltskin

7 characters

Mahlmann, Lewis. Aladdin, or the Wonderful Lamp
_____. Ali Baba and the 40 Thieves
_____. Baba Yaga
_____. King Midas and the Golden Touch
_____. Three Billy Goats Gruff
_____. Toads and Diamonds
_____. Uncle Remus Tales
Olfson, Lewy. The Braggart's Clever Wife

7 characters and extras

Bradley, Virginia. Beware of the Glump

8 characters

Mahlmann, Lewis. Cinderella
_____. The Emperor's Nightingale
_____. Puss in Boots
_____. The Rabbit Who Wanted Red Wings
_____. Rapunzel's Tower
_____. Snow White and Rose Red
Nolan, Paul T. Our Sister, Sitya
Traditional. Punch and Judy

9 characters

Bradley, Virginia. Shoes and Ships and a Mermaid
Mahlmann, Lewis. The Elephant's Child
_____. King of the Golden River
_____. The Legend of Urashima
_____. The Table, the Donkey and the Stick

9 characters and extras

Lynch-Watson, Janet. The Emperor's New Clothes

10 characters

Mahlmann, Lewis. The Blue Willow
_____. The Gingerbread Boy
_____. The Little Indian Brave

11 characters

Bradley, Virginia. Flat, Flat, Flat
Mahlmann, Lewis. Aesop's Fables

11 characters and extras

Mahlmann, Lewis. Beauty and the Beast
_____. Manora, the Bird Princess

12 characters

Mahlmann, Lewis. Sleeping Beauty
_____. Tale of Peter Rabbit

12 characters and extras

Mahlmann, Lewis. Perez and Martina

13 characters and extras

Harris, Aurand. Punch and Judy
Mahlmann, Lewis. The Nutcracker Prince
_____. The Pied Piper of Hamelin

16 characters and extras

Boiko, Claire. The Christmas Revel
Harris, Aurand. Pinocchio and the Fire-Eater

DIRECTORY OF PUBLISHERS

Abingdon Press
201 Eight Ave., S.
Nashville, TN   37202

Alternatives in Religious Education
3945 S. Oneida Street
Denver, Colorado   80237

Barnes, A. S., Inc.
9601 Aero Dr.
San Diego, CA   92123

Core Collection Books, Inc.
11 Middle Neck Rd.
Great Neck Rd.
Great Neck, NY   11021

Delacorte
One Dag Hammarskjold Plaza
New York, NY   10017

Dodd, Mead & Co.
79 Madison Ave.
New York, NY   10016

Doubleday & Co., Inc.
245 Park Ave.
New York, NY   10017

Elsevier Scientific Publishing Co.
52 Vanderbilt Ave.
New York, NY   10017

French, Samuel, Inc.
45 W. 25th St.
New York, NY   10010

Houghton Mifflin Co.
Two Park St.
Boston, MA   02108

Houghton Mifflin/Clarion Books
52 Vanderbilt Ave.
New York, NY 10017

Lothrop, Lee & Shepard Books
105 Madison Ave.
New York, NY   10016

McKay, David, Co. Inc.
Two Park Ave.
New York, NY   10016

Messner, Julian
Dist. by Simon and Schuster
1230 Ave. of the Americas
New York, NY   10020

Minnesota Press, University of
2037 University Ave. SE
Minneapolis, MN   55414

New Plays-Books Inc.
Box 273
Rowayton, CT   06853

Oak Tree Pubns. Inc.
9601 Aero Dr.
San Diego, CA   92123

Plays, Inc.
120 Boyston St.
Boston, MA   02116

Prentice-Hall, Inc.
Rte. 9W
Englewood Cliffs, NJ 07632

Scribner's, Charles, Sons
115 Fifth Ave.
New York, NY   10003

Seabury Press
810 Second Ave.
New York, NY   10017

Sterling Pub. Co., Inc.
Two Park Ave.
New York, NY   10016

University of Texas Press
P.O. Box 7819
Austin, TX   78713

Walker & Co.
720 5th Ave.
New York, NY   10019

BIBLIOGRAPHY OF COLLECTIONS

Anonymous. Kids Plays. Toronto: Playwright's Press, 1980. 185 pp. (ages 5-12) ISBN 0-8875-4165-8.

Abisch, Roz and Kaplan, Boche. The Make It, Play It, Show Time Book. New York: Walker and Co., 1977. 78 pp. (gr. 2-4). ISBN 0-8027-6286-5.

Alexander, Sue. Small Plays for Special Days. New York: Seabury Press, 1977. 64 pp. ISBN 0-8164-3184-1.

Alexander, Sue. Whatever Happened to Uncle Albert? New York: Houghton Mifflin, 1980. 94 pp. (elementary age). ISBN 0-395-29104-6.

Beck, Warren. Imagination, and Four Other One Act Plays for Boys and Girls. New York: Core Collection, 1977. 158 pp. (gr. 3-6). ISBN 77-89720.

Bradley, Alfred and Bond, Michael. Paddington on Stage. Boston: Houghton Mifflin, 1977. 112 pp. (gr. 2-5). ISBN 0-395-25155-9.

Bradley, Virginia. Holidays on Stage: A Festival of Special-Occasion Plays. New York: Dodd, Mead, 1981. 255 pp. (gr. 4-6). ISBN 0-396-07993-8.

Bradley, Virginia. Is There an Actor in the House? New York: Dodd, Mead, 1975. 298 pp. (gr. 4 up). ISBN 0-3960-7193-7.

Bradley, Virginia. Stage Eight; One-Act Plays. New York: Dodd, Mead, 1977. 234 pp. (gr. 7 up). ISBN 0-3960-7477-4.

Brown, Abbie Farwell. The Lantern, and Other Plays for Children. New York: Core Collection, 1978. 152 pp. (gr. 3-6). ISBN 0-8486-2033-X.

Carlson, Bernice. Let's Find the Big Idea. Nashville: Abingdon, 1982. 128 pp. (gr. 3-6). ISBN 0-687-21430-0.

Coleman, Jennings and Harris, Aurand, ed. Plays Children Love. New York: Doubleday, 1981. 678 pp. (gr. 3-adult). ISBN 0-385-17096-3.

Deary, Terence. Teaching Through Theatre: Six Practical Projects. New York: S. French, 1977. 49 pp. (ages 5-18). ISBN 0-573-09040-8.

DeRegniers, Beatrice Schenk. Picture Book Theater. New York: Clarion Books/Houghton Mifflin, 1982. unpaged. (gr. 1-3). ISBN 0-89919-061-8.

Donahue, John Clarke. The Cookie Jar and Other Plays. Minneapolis: University of Minneapolis Press, 1975. 178 pp. (gr. 5 up). ISBN 0-3166-0708-7.

Donahue, John Clark and Jenkins, Linda Walsh, ed. Five Plays from the Children's Theatre Company of Minneapolis. Minneapolis: University of Minnesota Press, 1975. 240 pp. (gr. 5 up). ISBN 0-8166-0711-7.

Fisher, Aileen. Bicentennial Plays and Programs. Boston: Plays Inc., 1975. 160 pp. (elementary--junior high). ISBN 0-8238-0185-3.

Gabriel, Michelle. Jewish Plays for Jewish Days. Denver: Alternatives in Religious Education, Inc., 1978. 92 pp. (gr. 3-6). no ISBN.

Gilfond, Henry. Walker Plays for Reading. New York: Walker & Co. 156 pp. (ages 12-16). ISBN 0-89187-475-5.

Harris, Aurand. Six Plays for Children. Austin: University of Texas Press, 1977. 378 pp. (gr. 4-6). ISBN 0-2927-0325-2.

Henderson, Nancy. Celebrate America: A Baker's Dozen of Plays. New York: Messner, 1978. 128 pp. (ages elementary--junior high). ISBN 0-671-32907-3.

Jagendorf, M. A., ed. One-Act Plays for Young Folks.

New York: Core Collection, 1977. (gr. 3-6). ISBN 0-8486-2028-3.

Kamerman, Sylvia, ed. Christmas Play Favorites for Young People. Boston: Plays, Inc., 1982. 283 pp. (elementary--junior and senior high). ISBN 0-8238-0257-4.

Kamerman, Sylvia, ed. Holiday Plays Around the Year. Boston: Plays, Inc., 1983. 291 pp. ISBN 0-8238-0261-2.

Kamerman, Sylvia, ed. On Stage for Christmas. Boston: Plays, Inc., 1978. 488 pp. (elementary--senior high). ISBN 0-8238-0226-4.

Kamerman, Sylvia, ed. Patriotic and Historical Plays for Young People. Boston: Plays, Inc., 1975. 262 pp. (gr. 6-10). ISBN 0-8238-0195-0.

Kamerman, Sylvia, ed. Space and Science Fiction Plays for Young People. Boston: Plays, Inc., 1981. 220 pp. (elementary--senior high). ISBN 0-8238-0252-3.

Kamerman, Sylvia, ed. Treasury of Christmas Plays. Boston: Plays, Inc., 1975. 509 pp. (elementary-senior high). ISBN 0-8238-0203-5.

Korty, Carol. Plays from African Folktales. New York: Scribner, 1969, 1975. 128 pp. (elementary). ISBN 0-684-14199-X.

Korty, Carol. Silly Soup: Ten Zany Plays With Songs and Ideas for Making Them Your Own. New York: Scribner, 1977. 148 pp. (elementary). ISBN 0-684-15171-5.

Kraus, Joanna Halpert. The Dragon Hammer and the Tale of Oniroko. Rowayton, CT: New Plays, Inc., 1977. 62 pp. (gr. 2-4). no ISBN.

Lynch-Watson, Janet. The Shadow Puppet Book. New York: Oak Tree Press, 1980. 128 pp. (gr. 3-6). ISBN 0-8069-7030-8.

Mahlmann, Lewis and Jones, David Cadwalader. Folk Tale Plays For Puppets. Boston: Plays, Inc., 1980. 142 pp. (gr. 3-6). ISBN 0-8238-0242-6.

Mahlmann, Lewis and Jones, David Cadwalader. Puppet
Plays from Favorite Stories. Boston: Plays, Inc.,
1977. 204 pp. (elementary). ISBN 0-8238-0219-1.

Marks, Burton and Rita. Puppet Plays and Puppet-Making.
Boston: Plays, Inc., 1982. 42 pp. (gr. 2-6). ISBN
0-8238-0256-6.

Martin, Judith. Everybody, Everybody. New York: Else-
vier/Nelson, 1981. 77 pp. (elementary). ISBN 0-5256-
6736-9.

McCaslin, Nellie. Puppet Fun. New York: McKay, 1977.
50 pp. (gr. K-3). ISBN 0-679-20416-4.

McSweeny, Maxine, ed. Christmas Plays for Young Players.
New York: A. S. Barnes, 1977, 149 pp. (gr. 4-8).
ISBN 0-4980-1959-4.

Murray, John. Modern Monologues for Young People. Boston: Plays, Inc., 1982. 150 pp. (gr. 6-12). ISBN
0-8238-0255-8.

Murray, John. Mystery Plays for Young Actors. Boston:
Plays, Inc., 1984. 188 pp. (middle-high school).
ISBN 0-8238-0265-5.

Nolan, Paul T. Folk Tale Plays Round the World. Boston:
Plays Inc., 1982. 248 pp. (gr. 5-up). ISBN 0-8238-
0253-1.

Olfson, Lewy. You Can Put on a Show. New York: Sterling, 1975. 144 pp. (gr. 2-4). ISBN 0-8069-7020-0.

Owen, Dilys. Play-Games. London: Muller, F., 1977.
72 pp. (gr. 1-3). ISBN 0-5846-2053-5.

Rembrandt, Elaine. Heroes, Heroines and Holidays. Denver: Alternatives in Religious Education, Inc., 1982.
148 pp. (gr. 5-12). ISBN 0-8670-5002-0.

Rockwell, Thomas. How to Eat Fried Worms and Other Plays.
New York: Delacorte Press, 1980. 142 pp. (gr. 3-6).
ISBN 0-440-03498-1.

Ross, Laura. Mask-Making with Pantomime and Stories from American History. New York: Lothrop, Lee and Shepard, 1975. 112 pp. (gr. 3-up). ISBN 0-6884-1721-3.

Warren, Lee. The Theater of Africa: An Introduction. Englewood Cliffs, NJ: Prentice-Hall, 1975. 112 pp. (gr. 5-up). ISBN 0-1321-9002-2.

Winther, Barbara. Plays from Folktales of Africa and Asia. Boston: Plays, Inc., 1976. 274 pp. ISBN 0-8238-0189-6.